A Conversation Book

Book II

A Conversation Book: English in Everyday Life

second edition

Tina Kasloff Carver
Sandra Douglas Fotinos

Northern Essex Community College
Haverhill, Massachusetts

Illustrated by
Paula Tatarunis
and
Don Martinetti

Prentice-Hall Englewood Cliffs, New Jersey 07632

Library of Congress Cataloging-in-Publication Data
(Revised for vol. 2)

Carver, Tina Kasloff, (date)
　A conversation book.

　　1. English language—Conversation and phrase books.
2. English language—Text-books for foreign speakers.
I. Fotinos, Sandra Douglas, (date)
PE1131.C43 1985　　　428.3′4　　　84-18290
ISBN　0-13-172362-6 (pbk. : v. 1)
ISBN　0-13-172370-7 (pbk. : v. 2)

Editorial/production supervision and
　interior design by Martha Masterson
Cover design: Lundgren Graphics, Ltd.
Manufacturing buyer: Harry P. Baisley

Chapter-opening Photo Credits:
1. Laimute E. Druskis;
2. United Nations, photo by S. Rotner;
3. Irene Springer;
4. Ken Karp;
5. Irene Springer;
6. Laimute E. Druskis;
7. Marc Anderson;
8. Ken Karp.

PRENTICE-HALL INTERNATIONAL (UK) LIMITED, *London*
PRENTICE-HALL OF AUSTRALIA PTY. LIMITED, *Sydney*
PRENTICE-HALL CANADA INC., *Toronto*
PRENTICE-HALL HISPANOAMERICANA, S.A., *Mexico*
PRENTICE-HALL OF INDIA PRIVATE LIMITED, *New Delhi*
PRENTICE-HALL OF JAPAN, INC., *Tokyo*
PRENTICE-HALL OF SOUTHEAST ASIA PTE. LTD., *Singapore*
EDITORA PRENTICE-HALL DO BRASIL, LTDA., *Rio de Janeiro*
WHITEHALL BOOKS LIMITED, *Wellington, New Zealand*

Dedicated to our parents:

Ruth and George Kasloff
Hertha and Earl Douglas

Contents

Communicating in English   1   Competency Objectives

Contents

Communicating in English   1   Competency Objectives

Family Life   2   Competency Objectives

Housing   3   Competency Objectives

4. Learn to use phone book to find services
5. Learn to use newspapr to find an apartment or house
6. Discuss real estate terms
7. Discuss what to look for when renting an apartment
8. Discuss moving and different options
9. Fill out change of address card
10. Identify furniture and appliances for different rooms of the home
11. Practice answering the door
12. Discuss home repairs and how to avoid accidents
13. Understand insurance and benefits of having insurance
14. Discuss landlord/tenant relationships; practice solving typical problems
15. Discuss problems with utilities
16. Understand difference between fahrenheit and centigrade; practice conversions

Employment   4

Competency Objectives

1. Discuss childhood ambitions
2. Identify jobs and job locations
3. Understand difference between *job title* and *job description*
4. Ask and answer common questions about classmates' jobs
5. Prepare, deliver, and evaluate speech about jobs
6. Discuss ways to find a job
7. Discuss wages
8. Discuss and practice proper behavior on the job interview
9. Practice filling out employment application
10. Discuss working conditions
11. Identify and discuss common problems at work
12. Discuss unemployment; practice filling out unemployment insurance form
13. Understand common banking terms
14. Practice filling out banking forms
15. Discuss use of checkbook; practice with checkbook entry and check
16. Understand basic terminology of taxes; discuss different forms of taxation
17. Understand benefits of social security
18. Learn how to apply for a social security card

Transportation and Travel   5

Competency Objectives

1. Identify different forms of commuting
2. Talk about traffic
3. Make a simple map and explain it
4. Take a survey about transporation; tabulate and discuss results
5. Learn to read a train and bus schedule
6. Identify parts of cars
7. Discuss preferences in selecting a car
8. Compare cars and driving in the U.S. and in native country
9. Discuss other vehicles and modes of transportation

10. Practice filling out a driver's license application
11. Discuss car maintenance
12. Discuss financing a car; understand terms on loan application
13. Understand and discuss car insurance and car accidents
14. Discuss traveling long distance
15. Prepare, deliver, and evaluate speech about a trip
16. Identify and discuss travel accommodations
17. Discuss tipping in hotels
18. Practice getting travel information from a travel agent
19. Understand differences in time zones

Health Care 6

Competency Objectives

1. Discuss differences in eating habits
2. Discuss good and bad health habits
3. Identify internal parts of human anatomy
4. Identify and explain health problems
5. Learn vocabulary for specialist physicians
6. Practice making doctor's appointment
7. Discuss quackery
8. Identify and discuss different clinics
9. Learn vocabulary for dental health
10. Compare dental care in U.S. and in native country
11. Identify items in pharmacy
12. Practice explaining needs to pharmacist
13. Identify and discuss equipment for first aid
14. Practice reading labels on medicine bottles
15. Discuss emergency situations and what to do
16. Discuss outpatient and emergency services
17. Learn about poisonous substances and how to deal with poison emergencies
18. Discuss immunizations
19. Learn vocabulary for health insurance
20. Discuss benefits of health insurance and life insurance

Consumer Information 7

Competency Objectives

1. Discuss ways to save money when shopping
2. Discuss shopping problems
3. Understand differences between metric and English measure; practice conversions
4. Practice talking to sales clerks when buying clothes
5. Discuss questions to be asked when shopping
6. Discuss returns and practice what to say when returning an item
7. Understand layaway; practice filling out layaway agreement
8. Discuss bargains; practice reading the newspaper for sales
9. Understand catalog sales; practice filling out catalog order form
10. Understand differences between guarantee and warranty; read cards and discuss
11. Discuss money management; cutting down expenses
12. Practice making a budget
13. Discuss consumer complaints

Values Clarification

8 Competency Objectives

1. Clarify personal values
2. Discuss cultural differences in values
3. Practice keeping a journal
4. Discuss the arts and talents of classmates
5. Read and discuss poetry in English and native languages of students
6. Understand and discuss funding for arts
7. Discuss high technology and its place in society
8. Discuss problems related to the environment
9. Discuss crime; clarify values related to law enforcement
10. Discuss punishment; clarify values on forms of punishment
11. Learn U.S. national anthem; compare anthems of students
12. Discuss voting in the U.S.; compare voting in native countries
13. Discuss government in the U.S. and in students' native countries
14. Discuss ethnic stereotyping and discrimination
15. Discuss education; compare education in the U.S. and in students' native countries
16. Clarify educational values
17. Practice talking to teachers about children's problems in school
18. Evaluate course; provide helpful suggestions for teacher
19. Evaluate own learning and future English language study needs

Appendix

INTRODUCTION

A CONVERSATION BOOK II is designed to develop the oral cross-cultural communication skills of intermediate-level students of English as a Second or Foreign Language. In the revised edition, we have retained the student-centered design and philosophy of the original book with increased emphasis on values clarification, structured group activities, communicative competencies and individualized vocabulary building.

When the activities of a conversation class are centered on the students themselves, natural language naturally develops. This is the basis for student-centered learning and teaching. The teacher in a student-centered classroom structures conversation activities, serves as a language and cross-cultural resource and provides guidance and support in completing the activities. The teacher facilitates the class, focusing it on the students, and maximizing student-talking time in every class session. Each student's contributions to the class are uniquely valuable. As the conversations are generated from the students' own lives and thoughts, each student becomes a resource for the class. Students take responsibility for their own learning as the teacher guides them towards their learning goals.

We would like to thank the students and teachers from many countries with whom we have talked over the years, whose conversations have inspired the content of this revision.

GUIDELINES FOR USING A CONVERSATION BOOK 2

How To Pair Students for Partners' Activities

It is simple to pair students sitting in front of, in back of, or beside each other. However, if you want to create new mixes in the class, here are two suggested ways.

1. Have students in the LEFT half of the class write their names on a slip of paper and fold it up. Collect the slips and have students in the RIGHT half of the class each pick one and find a partner. This works especially well at the beginning of the term. (Be sure to split the class evenly so everyone will have a partner.)

2. Have students make a list on the board of famous pairs of people (Romeo and Juliet), places (Tokyo and Japan), food (rice and beans) or antonyms (hot and cold). List enough pairs for exactly half of the class. Copy the list on a piece of paper and tear it into strips. Tear each strip in half and give one half to each student. Give students a specific amount of time to find their partners and sit down together.

How To Combine Students For Group Activities

The maximum number of students per group should not exceed FOUR. As with Partners' Activities, it is a good idea to vary the group mix. Some possibilities are:

1. Have students group themselves by horoscope sign.

2. Preselect students to mix native countries, native languages, sex, age, or other category appropriate to your class.
3. Have students count off by number.
4. Put students into pairs, then combine to form groups of four.

How To Time Activities

It is necessary to set a clear time limit on each activity before starting. The length of time given to each activity will depend on the kind of activity and how long you judge your students will take to complete it. For example, in an hour-long class, you might time your Partners' Activities like this:

1. Read and discuss questions with the whole class (10 minutes)
2. Pair students (5 minutes)
3. Allow interview (15-20 minutes, depending whether students take notes)
4. present interviews (15-20 minutes)
5. Wrap up and give assignment for next class (5 minutes)

Be prepared to be flexible at first, allowing for individual differences of each class. Make note of appropriate time limits for future reference.

How To Follow Through On Activities

The activities in this book are designed as goal-oriented tasks. While focusing on the learning process, they always lead toward a specific product, be it a report from a notetaker, a summation of a survey, a speech, or a role play. To insure student involvement in the activities, always follow through on the end goal.

1. Group students carefully.
2. Make sure instructions are clear.
3. Circulate, providing needed assistance, while students are working in pairs or groups.
4. Stick to time limits; save adequate time for reporting and summation.
5. Start the next class with a 5 minute review of the previous class. Assign a different student each time to present this review.

How To Establish A Supportive Class Environment

For establishing and maintaining a supportive climate, we have found it helpful to set groundrules:

1. Learning in this class is cooperative rather than competitive.
2. The teacher is also a learner in the class.
3. Each student's personal and cultural experiences are viewed as a unique resource for the class.
4. Teachers' and students' evaluation comments should be positive.
5. Criticism should always be constructive.
6. When dealing with controversial issues in the classroom, dogmatic statements should be rephrased. Use phrases that recognize individual perceptions such as, "This is how it looks to me because . . ." or "This is how it feels to me because . . ."

How To Evaluate Students' Oral Communication Skills

Although the traditional evaluator of students' skills is the instructor, experience indicates that instructors' perceptions are colored by familiarity with the students.

Therefore, we recommend using a combination of instructor evaluations, peer evaluations, and native-English speaking outsider evaluations.

1. Instructor Evaluations: written comments with specific recommendations seem to be most useful.

2. Peer Evaluations: have students take turns evaluating one another's speeches, oral reports, and audience behaviors formally by using the Speech Evaluation Forms and Audience Evaluation Forms in the Appendix. Encourage students to include positive comments. When they are finished, collect the forms, read them and give them to the student speaker. Have students provide informal evaluations when practicing speeches, reports and role plays with each other before presenting them to the whole class. Use these questions:

- Do you understand what I'm saying?
- Did I leave out anything? What?
- Should I change anything? What?

3. Native-English Speaker evaluations (NOT AN ESL TEACHER): informal native English speaker evaluations occur when students do community interviews or out-of-class surveys. After the activity has been completed, ask these questions in class:

- Did the native-English speaker understand you?
- Did you understand the native-English speaker?
- Was there a problem communicating? What happened?

Formal native-English speaker evaluations may be used for the students' final oral test. At Northern Essex Community College, an interview is videotaped and a native-English speaker from outside the ESL program (a content-course teacher, a counselor, or a community member) is invited to evaluate the videotape using the Oral Communication Evaluation form in the Appendix. A teacher from a higher level ESL course assists the native speaker in the evaluation process.

The conversation class should be a place where students feel comfortable communicating in English and develop an appreciation of their own and their classmates' backgrounds and culture. Students should look forward to their conversation class as a place to share and learn cooperatively.

Tina Kasloff Carver

Sandra Douglas Fotinos
Northern Essex Community College

Communicating in English

1

Getting Acquainted

Partners' Activity: Self-Portrait

Draw a picture of yourself. Sign your name on the drawing. Show it to your partner. Ask your partner if it looks like you. Explain your drawing to your partner.

Partners' Interview: Who Are You?

Ask your partner these questions. Introduce your partner to the class using the answers.

1. What is your name?
2. Where are you from?
3. What is your native language?
4. Tell me about your family.
5. When is your birthday?
6. Where would you like to be right now?
7. What is the most exciting thing that has happened to you in the past year?

Class Activity: Birthdays

Get a calendar for your classroom. Fill in everyone's birthday on the calendar. Check the calendar for birthdays every month and celebrate them with the class.

2

Introductions

Class Activity: Formal and Informal Introductions

List on the board formal and informal introductions in English. Copy them in your book. Discuss with your class appropriate situations for each kind of introduction.

FORMAL	*INFORMAL*
_____	_____
_____	_____
_____	_____

Group Activity: Introducing Yourself

Divide into groups of three or four students. Introduce yourself formally to your group and shake hands. Then introduce yourself informally.

Class Discussion: Cultural Differences

Look at the introduction pictured below. Do people ever greet each other this way where you come from? Show the class how people greet each other in your native country.

Class Activity: Saying Goodbye

List on the board formal and informal goodbyes in English. Copy them in your book. Discuss with your class appropriate situations for each kind of goodbye.

FORMAL	INFORMAL
_____	_____
_____	_____
_____	_____

Group Role Play: Hello and Goodbye

Role play these introductions with your group. Then present one introduction scene to the class.

1. Introduce your new friend to your mother or father. Talk for a minute. Then say goodbye.
2. Introduce your cousin to the teacher or the class. Talk for a minute. Then say goodbye.
3. Introduce two students to each other. Talk for a minute. Then say goodbye.
4. Introduce a group of people to each other at a party. Talk for a minute. Then say goodbye.

Class Activity: Alphabetize Names

Make an alphabetical list on the board of the names of all the students in your class. Write the surname (family name) first, then a comma, then the given name (first name). Which letters of the alphabet do most last names in your class begin with? Copy the list in your notebook.

Class Activity: Remembering Names

How many students' names do you remember in your class? Using the alphabetical list, point out each student on the list and say something special that you remember about that student.

Class Discussion: Special Names

Discuss these questions with your class.

1. Do any members of the class have the same name? Who?
2. Is anyone here named after a relative? What relative?
3. Is anyone here named after a famous person? What famous person?
4. Has anyone here changed his or her name? Why? What was it before?
5. Does anyone's name mean something special? What does it mean?
6. Who has the longest name in the class? The shortest?
7. Whose name is the most difficult to pronounce? The easiest?

Where Are You From?

Class Activity: Native Countries

Find your native country on this map.* Show your classmates where you are from.

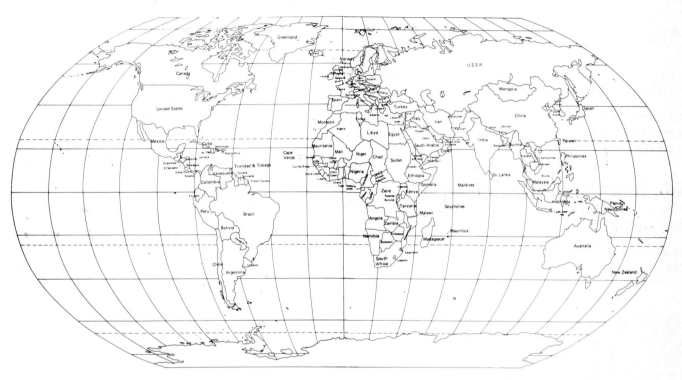

By permission of Prentice-Hall, Inc.

On the Board: Nationalities

Make a list on the board of all the nations and nationalities represented in your class. Then make a list of other nations on the map and the nationalities of each. How many nations and nationalities do you know?

Example:	**Nation**	**Nationality**
	U.S.A.	American
	England	English
	Spain	Spanish
	_____	_____
	_____	_____

*Or use a map of your country. Show where you grew up.

Speech: Your Native Country

Prepare a brief speech for your class about your native country. Try to answer these questions in your speech. Add more information too. Practice with a small group before you present your speech to the class. You may use note cards, but do not read your speech.

1. Where is your country (hemisphere, continent, in relation to other countries)?
2. What is its population?
3. What is the capital city?
4. What kind of currency is used?
5. What languages do people speak?
6. What seasons are there? What is the weather like?
7. What kind of government is there?
8. What religions are practiced?
9. _____

Speech and Audience Evaluation

Choose four students to evaluate each speech. Choose one student to evaluate the audience. Use the speech and audience evaluation forms on page 175 of the Appendix. You may duplicate these forms as many times as is necessary.

What Do You Like to Do?

Find Someone Who . . .

Find someone in your class who fits each description. Write the name of an appropriate student for each description. When everyone is finished, compare answers.

1. _____ likes to watch TV.

2. _____ likes to play soccer.

3. _____ likes to dance.

4. _____ likes to go to the beach.

5. _____ likes to swim.

6. _____ likes to listen to music.

7. _____ likes to read.

8. _____ likes to travel.

9. _____ likes to stay at home.

10. _____ likes to talk on the telephone.

Class Activity: Who Am I?

On an index card, write three unusual things that you like to do or that you have done. Do not write your name. The teacher will collect the cards and read each one aloud. Try to guess who wrote each card. (The teacher should include one too!)

Class Activity: Games

What are these people doing? Are any board games or card games popular in your native country? Where do people sit to play them? What games do you know? Bring a game to the next class. Teach the class how to play.

Please

On the Board: Polite Requests

Look at these pictures. Make a list on the board of other polite ways to ask these questions. Copy the questions in your book.

Asking for Directions

Asking for the Time

Group Role Play: Polite Requests

Role play the scenes above with your group. Then present one scene to the class.

Offer and Invite

Class Activity: Offers and Invitations

With your class, add to these situations. (Offer something and invite someone.) Then discuss the differences between offering or inviting a stranger or a friend, an old person or a young person.

Offering

1. Ask if you can help a teacher carry a big pile of books.
2. Offer a friend a ride home.
3. Offer to help a child who seems to be lost.
4. _____
5. _____

Inviting

1. Invite a friend to join you at a table.
2. Invite a classmate for a cup of coffee.
3. Invite someone you don't know to play a game you are playing (cards, soccer, baseball, etc.).
4. _____
5. _____

Partners' Role Play: Offering or Inviting

With a partner, role play one of the situations above for the class.

Community Activity: Guest Speaker

Invite a speaker to your class. Discuss with your class who you would like to have come to speak to your class. Compose a letter on the board inviting that person to speak. Send the letter and see if the speaker accepts your invitation.

Group Role Play: A Dinner Party

With your group, role play a dinner party. Choose one person to be the host or hostess. Before you present your role play to the class, make a list on the board of everything you will put on the table. Be very specific. In the role play, use the vocabulary from the board to make polite invitations, offers, and requests. Be very polite.

Class Discussion: Cultural Differences in Dinner Parties

What are the customs for entertaining guests at dinner in your native country? Explain to the class.

Thank You

Group Activity: Thank You Note

Read this thank you note with your group. Then think of someone you would like to thank. Write a short note.
Explain the situation to your group. Read the note to the group.

October 21, 1987

Dear Susan,

Thanks very much for the beautiful flowers. Yellow roses and daisies are my favorites. I wish you could see them. They make the hospital room so bright and cheerful.

I'm feeling better already.

Love,
Debbie.

———————— , ————

———————— ,

————————————————————

————————————————————

————————————————————

————————————————— .

————————————————————

————————————————————

————————————————————

————————————————————

————————————————— .

———————— ————

————————————

On the Board: You're Welcome

*How do you say **thank you** and **you're welcome** in your native language? Write the words on the board. Teach the class how to pronounce them.*

Class Discussion: Different Ways to Say Thank You

In your native country, what is the custom for saying thank you:

> for a pleasant evening?
> for a gift?
> for a favor?

How do the customs for expressing gratitude in your country differ from those of the United States?

Polite and Impolite Behavior

Group Discussion: Waiting in Line; Listening to a Speaker

Choose a note taker for your group to take notes on your discussion and to read the notes to the whole class afterwards.

Waiting in Line

- Do people wait in lines where you live?
- Where do they wait in lines?
- How do you behave in line?
- How do you think people should behave in line?
- Did you ever see anyone do anything strange in a line? What happened?
- Are there any differences between behavior in lines in your native country and in the United States?

Listening to a Speaker

- What is polite behavior when you are listening to a speaker?
- What is impolite behavior?
- Are there any differences between polite behavior in your native country and in the United States?
- What do people do to show their appreciation to a speaker?
- What do they do if they don't like the speech?

Partners' Role Play: Being Polite

Read these scenes with your partner. Pick one and role play the skit for the class. Then discuss the role play with the class. Was your behavior polite or impolite?

1. You are listening to a speech and the person next to you is making noise. You can't hear the speaker. What do you do?
2. You are in a crowded movie theater and the person in front of you has a big hat on. What do you do and say?
3. You want to get out of your parking space but your car is blocked by a delivery truck. What do you do and say?
4. You want to pass through a crowd. What do you do and say?
5. You are waiting in a line at the bank. Someone cuts into line in front of you. What do you do and say?

Group Discussion: Different Perceptions

What do you think is happening in these pictures? Discuss them with your group. Compare answers with those of other groups.

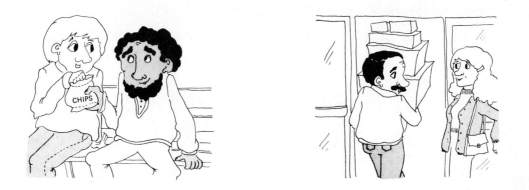

Class Discussion: Differences in Polite and Impolite Behavior

Many times behavior seems impolite. This is because of cultural differences; what is considered impolite in one culture may not be impolite in another culture. What experiences have you had with behavior you find unusual? Tell the class.

15

Apologizing

Class Discussion: Different Ways to Apologize

Match these pictures with the apologies below. Discuss what is happening in each picture.

_____ I'm sorry to keep you waiting.

_____ Excuse me, please. May I speak with you for a moment?

_____ I beg your pardon. I didn't understand what you said. Could you repeat it, please?

_____ I'm sorry. I have to leave now.

_____ Can you ever forgive me, darling?

_____ Oh! I'm sorry! Are you all right?

Group Role Play: Practicing Apologies

With your group, choose one of these scenes to role play. Then present your skit to the class.

1. You bump into someone.
2. You want to interrupt someone who is busy.
3. You have to leave. Apologize and explain why you must go.
4. You are late to class. Apologize and explain.
5. The cashier forgot to give you change. Ask for it.
6. You don't understand someone. Apologize and ask him to repeat.

Telephone Communication

Find Someone Who . . .

Find someone in your class who fits each description. Write the name of an appropriate student for each description. When everyone is finished, compare answers.

1. _____ has used a pay phone at an airport.

2. _____ has a telephone calling card.

3. _____ has made a call to another country.

4. _____ has had a problem with a phone call.

5. _____ has used the telephone on the job.

6. _____ has dialed a wrong number.

Class Discussion: Calls to and from Your Native Country.

Have you ever called your native country from the United States or called the United States from your native country? How much did the call cost? How did you make the phone call? Did you dial direct or did the operator assist you? What time of day did you call? Tell the class about how you made the call.

Partners' Activity: Wrong Number

Situation: This woman got out of the bathtub to answer the phone. It was a wrong number.

1. Fill in the bubble with your partner. What is she saying?

2. Write a caption under the picture. What is she thinking?

3. Share your ideas with the class.

_____

_____

17

Partners' Activity: Unwanted Calls

This is a conversation between a magazine salesman and a housewife. Finish the dialog with your partner and present it to the class.

Telephone rings.

WOMAN: Hello.
MAGAZINE SALESMAN: Good morning, madam. Are you the lady of the house?
WOMAN: Yes, I am.
MAGAZINE SALESMAN: This is your lucky morning. I have a wonderful offer for you. If you will listen to me tell you about ten magazines, I will give you a very special gift when you buy them.

WOMAN: _____
MAGAZINE SALESMAN: _____
_____
WOMAN: _____
MAGAZINE SALESMAN: _____

Class Discussion: Handling Unwanted Calls

Have you ever had an unwanted call or a call you didn't understand? Tell the class about it.

Communication Problems

Group Problem Solving: Lack of Communication

Urban life and high technology create some communication problems. What is happening in these pictures? Discuss them in small groups and think of things these people could do to solve their communication problems. Report your suggestions to the class.

Community Activity: Conversation in English

Find someone in your community (outside your English class) who speaks English. Talk with a native speaker if possible. Talk about anything. Report your conversation to the class.

2

Family Life

Families

Extended Family

BELOVED HUSBAND

Group Discussion: Families

Choose a note taker for your group to take notes on your discussion and read the notes to the whole class afterwards.

1. Immediate families include only a father, mother, and children. How many immediate families are in the extended family picture?
2. Do people in your native country usually live together in immediate or extended family units?
3. If an extended family lives together, who is usually included? Who is the head of the household?
4. Do you prefer to live in an immediate or an extended family group? Why?
5. How many children do families usually have in your native country? What is considered a large family?
6. Who in your group comes from the largest immediate family? The smallest?
7. In the extended family picture, do you know the vocabulary for all the relationships? Where is the great-grandfather? The stepmother? The twins? The ex-husband? The great aunt? The second cousin? Identify all the relationships.
8. Does anyone in your group still have a great-grandparent living? How old is he or she?
9. Do any students in your group have twins in their family? Triplets? Quadruplets? Quintuplets?

Partners' Activity: Your Family Tree

Draw your own family tree. Explain it to your partner. Then ask your partner these questions.

1. Are you married? What is your wife's (husband's) name?
2. Do you have any children? How many? How old are they? What are their names?
3. How many brothers and sisters do you have? How old are they? Where do they live? Are they married?
4. Do you have any nephews and nieces? How many?
5. Are your parents living? Where do they live? Are your grandparents living? When did they pass away (die)?

Getting Married

Class Vocabulary Activity: Getting Married in the United States

Read this information with your class and discuss the vocabulary.

Every state in the United States has its own **legal requirements** for marriage. All states require a **marriage license**. A **blood test** is also required in most states.

There is a **minimum age** for marrying in all 50 states. With parental consent, in some states, the legal age for females is 14, for males, 16. The age requirement is higher in most states.

In the United States, a couple may be married in either a **religious** or a **civil ceremony**. Many young people decide by themselves whether to get married or not. They do not usually ask their parents for permission if they are over the legal age. Sometimes they **elope** and do not tell their parents until after they are already married.

Some people have big weddings; others have simple weddings. They take their **vows** before a **judge** or a **justice-of-the-peace** with two other people as **legal witnesses**.

It is customary for a wife to wear a **wedding ring** on her left hand. Some husbands also wear wedding rings if they want to. A **widow** or **widower** usually wears a wedding ring, but a **divorcé** does not.

Group Discussion: Customs in Your Native Country

Choose a note taker for your group to take notes on your discussion and to read the notes to the whole class afterwards.

1. Do young people in your native country ask their parents for permission to marry?
2. Is a religious ceremony legal in your native country? Is a civil ceremony legal there?
3. Who wears a wedding ring in your native country? What finger and hand do people wear their wedding rings on?
4. In your native country, where do couples usually live after they get married? (Alone? With the husband's family? With the wife's family?)
5. In your native country, at what ages do women customarily marry? At what ages do men customarily marry?
6. In the United States, it is illegal to be married to two people at the same time. A man with two wives or a woman with two husbands is a *bigamist*. Is it legal to be married to more than one person at a time in your native country?

Wedding Customs

Partners' Activity: Getting Engaged and Getting Married in the United States

With your partner, describe what is happening in each of these pictures. Write a caption for each frame. Compare your captions with those of the rest of the class.

Class Discussion: Weddings in Your Native Country

Discuss these questions with your class.

1. When a couple gets engaged in your native country, does the young man give his fiancée a diamond ring? What are your traditional engagement customs?

2. Do friends of the bride give her showers? What kinds of presents do people give to engaged couples? What do they give to the bride and groom when they get married?

3. Is there a reception after the wedding? Is wedding cake served? What else do people do at the reception?

4. Do newlyweds go on a honeymoon? Where do they commonly go?

Poll the Class: Modern Marriages

What do you think of marriage today? Read these statements together. List two more.

Find out how many students in your class agree or disagree with these statements about marriage. Write the results of your poll on the board. Discuss the results with the class.

	Agree	Disagree
Marriage is better today than it was 100 years ago.		
Being married is better than being single.		
If two single people love each other, they should get married and not worry about marriage problems.		

Having a Baby

Class Discussion: Preparing for a Baby

Match the pictures with the sentences below. Discuss the pictures with your class. How do these customs differ in your native country?

 1 A pregnant woman in the United States usually goes to an obstetrician once a month for a prenatal checkup.

 2 Stores sell many attractive maternity clothes.

 3 Friends of the mother-to-be often give her a baby shower.

 4 Many hospitals allow a husband to stay with his wife in the delivery room.

 5 The new father hands out cigars to everyone he sees: pink ribbon on the cigar for a girl, blue ribbon on the cigar for a boy.

Group Discussion: Babies in Your Native Country

Choose a note taker for your group to take notes on your discussion and to read the notes to the whole class afterwards.

1. Who delivers babies in your country? An obstetrician? A midwife?

2. Do most parents want to have sons or daughters in your native country? Why? Which do your prefer? Why?

3. A song to put a baby to sleep is a lullaby. Do you know a lullaby in your native language? Sing it to the group.

Husbands and Wives

Group Discussion: Changing Roles

This picture illustrates changing roles in the American family. Choose a note taker for your group to take notes on your discussion and to read the notes to the whole class afterwards.

1. What is happening?
2. Why is it happening?
3. Is it happening in your family?
4. How do you feel about this change?
5. In your native country, what does it mean to be the head of the family?
6. Describe the roles of husbands and wives in your native country.

Group Role Play: Solving a Family Problem

With your group, find a solution to this problem. Present your skit to the class.

A mother has returned to school to complete her education. She has a lot of studying to do, and she can't manage all the housework anymore. Her husband and two teenaged children want her to be happy, but they don't like dirty laundry and TV dinners. What can they do?

Class Role Play: Common Conflicts Between Husbands and Wives

With your class, add to this list of common things that husbands and wives argue about. Choose students to role play the conflicts for the class.

1. The husband thinks his wife is spending too much money on clothes.
2. The wife thinks her mother-in-law is too bossy.
3. _____
4. _____

Bringing Up Children

Partners' Interview: Role Models

Ask your partner these questions. Report your interview to the class.

WHAT'S THAT ON YOUR NECK, DAD?

1. In this picture, the father is serving as a role model for his son, showing him how men dress. Can you remember how your father or mother dressed when you were a child? Do you dress that way now? Why or why not?

2. What do you remember learning from your father or your mother? In what ways are you like your father or your mother today?

Class Discussion: Communicating with Children

1. What is happening in this picture?
2. Many Americans blame family communication problems on too much television. Do you agree or disagree? Why?
3. What can parents do with their children to guard against this problem?
4. List on the board things parents can do with their children to avoid this problem.

Community Activity: Advice Columns

Find advice columns in an English language newspaper. Bring the columns to class. Read them together. Do you agree or disagree with the advice?

Teenagers

On the Board: Concerns about Teenagers

Make a list on the board of problems parents of teenagers sometimes worry about. Decide with your class which problem is the most serious. Label it (1). Number the rest of the worries on the list in order of seriousness.

Group Discussion: Solving Teenagers' Problems

Discuss these situations with your group. What do you think the parents should do? Choose a note taker for your group to take notes on your discussion and to read the notes to the whole class afterwards.

1. Your sixteen-year-old daughter wants to go to a drive-in movie with her eighteen-year-old boyfriend who drives a car. What should you say?
2. Your seventeen-year-old son has a twelve o'clock curfew. He thinks this is unreasonable because most of his friends do not have any curfew at all. What should you say?
3. Your teenaged children's bedrooms are always very messy. They seem to like them that way. What should you do?
4. You think your sixteen-year-old son may be using drugs. What should you do?
5. Choose another problem from the list on the board to discuss.

Role Play: Independence or Rebellion?

Discuss these situations with your group. Are these young people asserting their independence or rebelling against their parents or both? Can you find a good solution? Choose one situation to role play for the whole class.

An eighteen-year-old daughter has decided to leave home. She wants to live in an apartment with a friend. Her parents do not want her to go. Her younger brother and sister do not know what to think.

A sixteen-year-old son wants to quit school and go to work and marry his girlfriend. His family is upset.

Poll the Class: What Do You Think of Teenagers Today?

Read these statements together. List two more. Find out how many members of your class agree and disagree with the following statements about teenagers. Write the results of your poll on the board. Discuss the results with the class.

	Agree	Disagree
Teenagers today have more problems than teenagers had twenty-five years ago.		
Most of the teenagers I know are responsible, thoughtful people.		
Teenagers should have the right to dress the way they want to.		

31

Grandparents

Class Discussion: Moving Away

Discuss these questions with your class.

1. What is happening in this picture? This happens very often in the United States. Does it happen often in your native country?

2. How many members of your class have lived with their grandparents? How many have lived near their grandparents?

3. What are advantages of living close to grandparents? What are disadvantages? Make a list on the board.

Group Role Play: Solving a Family Problem

With your group, role play this situation for the class. In your scene, find a solution for this problem. Present your skit to the class.

This woman's mother is a widow. She lives alone in a large house which she cannot afford to take care of. If she moves in with her daughter's family, her two granddaughters will have to share a room. The husband does not get along well with his mother-in-law. What can this family do?

32

Divorce

Class Vocabulary Activity: Divorce in the United States

Read this information and discuss the vocabulary.

The **divorce rate** is rising in the United States. In 1960, for every four marriages there was one divorce. Twenty years later, for every two marriages there was one divorce.

Every state in the United States has its own divorce laws. There are many different grounds for **divorce**. A few states have **no-fault divorce laws** in which the grounds are **irreconcilable differences**. Some other grounds for divorce in different states are **adultery, cruelty, desertion, alcoholism, impotence, felony conviction, neglect to provide, incurable insanity, bigamy, separation, and drug addiction.**

There are also different **residency requirements**. In most states the residency requirement before you can get a divorce is one year. In some, the requirement is six weeks.

Many couples go to a **marriage counselor** before they decide to separate. The marriage counselor tries to help them solve their problems.

Group Discussion: Divorce in Your Native Country

Choose a note taker for your group to take notes on your discussion and to read the notes to the whole class afterwards.

1. Do couples with marital problems ever go to a marriage counselor in your native country? If not, to whom do they go for help?
2. Is divorce legal in your native country? What grounds for divorce are allowed? Is it easy to get a divorce in your native country? What is the procedure?
3. What problems arise from divorce? Do you know anyone who has been divorced? Are they better off divorced? Why or why not?
4. When couples take marriage vows, they promise to remain together:

   for better, for worse,
   for richer, for poorer,
   in sickness and in health,
   'till death do us part.

   Nevertheless, the divorce rate is rising. Why do you think this is happening?

34

3

Housing

City and Country Living

Group Activity: Pictures for Comparison

With your group, make a list of all the differences you can find between the picture of the apartment building in the city and the picture of the house in the country. Check your answers on page 170 of the Appendix.

City Home

Country Home

Find Someone Who . . .

Find someone in your class who fits each category. Report your answers to the class.

1. _____ prefers city life.

   What city? _____

2. _____ prefers country life.

   How far away from a city or town? _____

3. _____ has had a vegetable garden.

   What vegetables? _____

4. _____ has grown flowers.

   What kinds? What colors? _____

5. _____ has had a pet.

   What kind of animal? What was its name? _____

Class Discussion: City Life versus Country Life

Discuss with your class the advantages and disadvantages of city and country life. Make lists on the board under these headings:

ADVANTAGES		DISADVANTAGES	
City Life	**Country Life**	**City Life**	**Country Life**
_____	_____	_____	_____
_____	_____	_____	_____
_____	_____	_____	_____

Poll the class to find out how many prefer city life and how many prefer country life.

Speech: City or Natural Wonder

Prepare a speech for your class on a city or a natural wonder in your native country. Try to answer these questions in your speech. Practice with a small group before you present the speech to the class. You may use note cards, but do not read the speech.

City Outline

1. Name of the city in English; name in your native language
2. Size
3. History
4. Famous landmarks
5. Why you like it
6. _____

Natural Wonder Outline

1. Kind of natural wonder (volcano, mountain, waterfall, etc.)
2. Name in English; name in your native language
3. Description
4. History
5. Why you like it
6. _____

Speech and Audience Evaluation

Choose four students to evaluate each speech. Choose one student to evaluate the audience. Use the Speech and Audience Evaluation Forms on page 175 of the Appendix.

Services

Group Discussion: City and Town Services

Choose a note taker for your group to take notes on your discussion and to read the notes to the whole class afterwards.

1. If you live in a city, what day is your trash collected?
2. Do you put trash and garbage in the same container?
3. What is the difference between trash and garbage?
4. Does your city have separate collections for paper? Glass? Tin or aluminum cans?
5. Does your building have an incinerator? A compactor?
6. If you live in the country, do you take your trash to a dump? What else do you do with your garbage?

7. Is your water good to drink? Is it city water? Does it come from a well? What do you do if your water is dirty?
8. Do you have a septic tank for sewage?
9. What are the men doing in these pictures?
10. Look in your local telephone directory under the name of your city or town to see what services are listed there. Make a list on the board.

Looking for Housing

Class Vocabulary Activity: Classified Advertisements

In the United States, if you are looking for an apartment or a house, look in the newspaper classified section or visit a real estate broker. Read these classified advertisements with your class. Discuss the abbreviations and the vocabulary.

APARTMENTS FOR RENT

ALLSTON: 1-2-3 bdrm. apts, moderate rents. $450 up. Mod. kits. & baths. 555-8492

ARLINGTON: mod. studio apt.; clean bldg.; sep. kit.; elev., $125/wk. 555-4069

BELMONT: 3 rm. furn. apt. lg. kit.; nr. trans.; pkg., ht. & hw. incl.; yard fencd. $600. 555-1928

EVERETT: Htd. 3 & 4 rm. apts. avail. 9/1, $420-$650. Supt. 555-0019

HILLDALE: 2-bdrm., very sunny apt. duplex. New kit. w. dw. $650 htd. 555-2285

MILLTOWN: Mod. apt., nr. shops, transp.; balc.; util. not incl.; avail. now
    Studio, $395
    1-Bdrm, $475
    2-Bdrm, $550
Cranton Realty; 555-4739

NORTON: Furn. studio apt. w. all util. $300. 555-2940. No pets. Adult only.

REAL ESTATE

AMESTON: $74,000 3-bdrm. ranch; frpl., livrm., dinrm., kit., partly finished. bsmt. For more info, call Amestown Realtors, Inc. 555-8501

BRADFORD: sales & rentals. GEORGE J. JONES, REALTOR, 384 Main St., 555-4720

BRADFORD: bank foreclosure, 4-bdrm. 2½ bath, ww cpt., 2-car gar. $181,000. CRAIG & DAWSON, 555-3390

CLAYVILLE: 2 fam. w. charm; renov. kits., 6rms. plus 4 rms. on 3d flr.; gar., ¼ acre. $185,000. DELANO REALTY 555-2289

DANTON: $109,000. "Desperate" owner "must sell" 6-rm. ranch. 3 or 4 bdrms. Beautiful lot w. trees. Assume 12% annual percentage rate mortgage; VA buyers welcome. Call now. WELLS REAL ESTATE, 555-3388

CLASSIFIED ADVERTISEMENT ABBREVIATIONS

apt.	apartment	info.	information
avail.	available	kit.	kitchen
balc.	balcony	lg.	large
bdrm.	bedroom	livrm.	living room
bldg.	building	loc.	location
bsmt.	basement	mod.	modern
dinrm.	dining room	nr.	near
dw.	dishwasher	pkg.	parking
elev.	elevator	renov.	renovated
fam.	family	rm.	room
flr.	floor	sep.	separate
frpl.	fireplace	supt.	superintendent
furn.	furnished	trans.	transportation
gar.	garage	util.	utilities
htd.	heated	w.	with
hw.	hot water	ww. cpt.	wall-to-wall carpet
incl.	included		

Class Discussion: Finding an Apartment or House

Discuss these questions with your class.

1. Why are some apartments and houses more expensive than others?
2. In most parts of the United States the kitchen is considered a room but the bathroom isn't. A three-room apartment is an apartment with a kitchen, a bathroom, a living room and a bedroom. What is a four-room apartment? How are rooms counted in your native country?
3. What is a *lease*? Did you ever have to sign a lease when you rented an apartment? What were the terms?
4. What is a *deposit*? Did you ever have to put down a deposit when renting an apartment? How much? What was it for?
5. How do people find apartments and houses in your native country?

Community Activity: Looking at Ads in the Newspaper

Bring in the local newspaper and practice reading more ads for apartments and homes. How many other abbreviations can you find? What do they mean?

Partners' Activity: Your Home

Ask your partner these questions about his or her home. Write Y (yes) or N (no) next to each question.

KITCHEN: Sink: _____ Is it large enough to wash dishes in?

_____ Does it drain properly?

_____ Does it leak?

Refrigerator: _____ Did you have to buy your refrigerator?

_____ Does the refrigerator work?

_____ Does the freezer work?

Ventilation: _____ Is there adequate ventilation?

_____ Does the kitchen have a window?

BATHROOM: Toilet: _____ Does it flush?

_____ Does it leak?

Sink: _____ Does it leak?

Tub and Shower: _____ Does the tub hold water?

_____ Is it stained?

_____ Does the shower drip?

Ventilation: _____ Does the bathroom have a window?

GENERAL CONDITION: Walls: _____ Are they made of easily cleaned material?

_____ Can you hang things on the wall?

_____ Can you hear your neighbors through the walls?

Water: _____ Is there enough hot and cold water every day?

Heat: _____ Is it adequate?

_____ Are you responsible for the heating bills?

_____ Is the heating equipment in good condition?

_____ If you have space heaters, are they in good condition?

Electricity and Wiring: _____ Are there separate outlets for each room?

_____ Are there light fixtures in the ceiling in each room?

CONDITION OF BUILDING: Fixtures: _____ Is there a working light fixture in the:

_____ hallways?

_____ stairways?

_____ storage area?

_____ front of the building?

Wiring: _____ Is there any temporary wiring in the building?

Moving

Group Discussion: Moving Experiences

Choose a note taker for your group to take notes on your discussion and to read the notes to the whole class afterwards.

1. What is happening in this picture?
2. How many times have you moved?
3. What are some problems you have had in moving?
4. If you have many things to move, do you prefer to hire a moving company or to rent a truck and move yourself? Why?

Class Vocabulary Activity: Having Your Mail Forwarded

When you move in the United States you can have your mail delivered to your new home even though it is addressed to your old one. You must fill out a change of address card at the post office. Read this card with your class, then fill it out. How long will the post office forward mail to you? For how long will the post office forward magazines and newspapers?

	Print or Type *(Last Name. First Name. Middle Initial)*		
THIS ORDER PROVIDES for the forwarding of First-Class Mail for a period not to exceed 18 months. All parcels of obvious value will be forwarded for a period not to exceed one year.			
CHANGE OF ADDRESS IS FOR: ☐ Firm ☐ **Entire Family** *(When last name of family members differ, separate orders for each last name must be filed.)* ☐ **Individual Signer Only**	**OLD ADDRESS** — No. and St., Apt., Suite P.O. Box R.D. No. Box Post Office State ZIP Code		
I agree to pay forwarding postage for newspapers and magazines for 90 days. ☐ No ☐ Yes	**NEW ADDRESS** — No. and St., Apt., Suite P.O. Box R.D. No. Box Post Office State ZIP Code		
USPS USE ONLY Clerk/Carrier Endorsement			
Carrier Route Number	Effective Date		If Temporary, Expiration Date
Date Entered	Sign Here X		Date Signed

PS FORM 3575. JAN. 1984   *Signature & title of person authorizing address change. (DO NOT print or type.)*

Redecorating Your Living Room

Partners' Activity: Living Room Furniture

Partner A

1. Look at the living room picture on page 178 of the Appendix.
2. Tell Partner B what is in the living room and where each item is.
3. Don't look at Partner B's picture until it is finished.

Partner B

1. Look at this page only.
2. Draw the items on this page as Partner A describes them.
3. When your picture is finished, compare it to page 178 of the Appendix.
4. Share your drawing with the class.

Group Discussion: Your Ideal Living Room

If you could decorate your living room any way you wanted, what would you have in it? Draw your ideal living room. Describe it to the group.

Model Kitchens

Partners' Activity: Differences in Kitchens

Partner A looks only at this picture. Partner B looks only at the kitchen picture on page 177 in the Appendix. Make a list together of the differences between the two kitchens. Don't look at both pictures together until you have completed your list. Compare your lists with those of the rest of the class.

Find Someone Who . .

Add five more kitchen questions. Then find someone in your class who fits each category.

1. _____ has a kitchen with a window.

2. _____ eats at a kitchen table.

3. _____ has a blender in the kitchen.

4. _____ has a gas stove.

5. _____ doesn't have enough storage space in the kitchen.

6. _____

7. _____

8. _____

9. _____

10. _____

Who Comes to Your Door?

Group Activity: Answering the Door

What would you say to these people if they came to your door? Finish the dialogs. Read your dialogs to the rest of the class.

Little boy: Can I have a drink of water, please?
You: _____

Brush salesman: Good morning, I'd like to show you some of our new brushes, ma'am.
You: _____

Delivery man: Would you sign here, please?
You: _____

Exterminator: You called for an exterminator?
You: _____

Partners' Role Play: People at Your Door

Who else comes to your door? What do you say to them? With your partner choose one of the following situations, or make up your own. Prepare a conversation. Present your skit to the class.

1. a neighbor who wants to borrow something
2. a salesman of magazines, vacuum cleaners, cosmetics, candy, etc.
3. a bill collector
4. a TV repairman, plumber, electrician, painter
5. someone collecting for charity
6. _____

Home Repair Problems

Group Activity: Handyman Mistakes

What is happening in these strip stories? Discuss them with your group. Write captions for each frame. Then decide how you would make these repairs and what mistakes these people made. Read your captions and your solutions to the class.

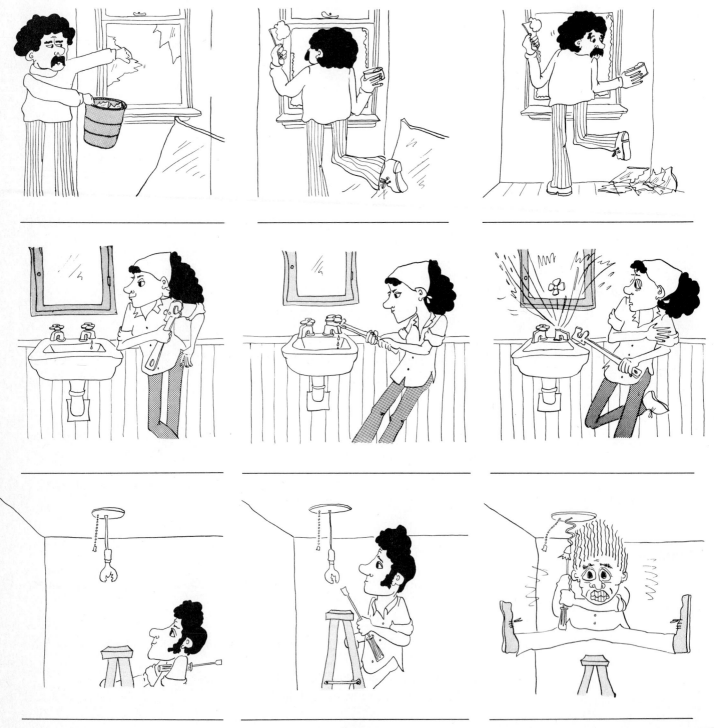

Group Discussion: Your Home Repairs

Have you ever done any home repairs? Tell your group about it. Have you ever had an accident doing home repairs? Tell your group about it. Report to the class on your discussion.

Class Discussion: Doing Your Own Repairs

In the United States, many people do their own home repairs. Is it the same in your native country? Why do you think Americans like to do these things? Is it considered undignified in your native country to do home repairs and housework?

Class Discussion: Amateur Repairman

What do you think this man is doing? What is his profession?

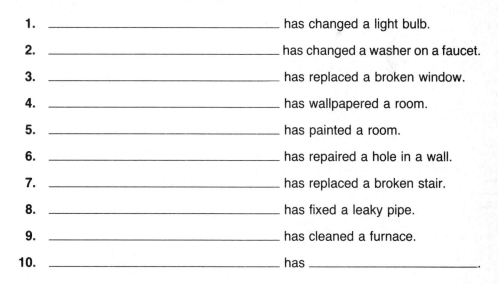

Find Someone Who . . .

Find someone in your class who fits each description. Share your answers with the class.

1. _____ has changed a light bulb.

2. _____ has changed a washer on a faucet.

3. _____ has replaced a broken window.

4. _____ has wallpapered a room.

5. _____ has painted a room.

6. _____ has repaired a hole in a wall.

7. _____ has replaced a broken stair.

8. _____ has fixed a leaky pipe.

9. _____ has cleaned a furnace.

10. _____ has _____.

Insurance

Class Discussion: Your Insurance

Discuss these questions with your class.

1. Why is it important to have insurance if you rent an apartment?
2. Why is it important to have insurance if you own a home?
3. Was your home ever robbed? What was taken?
4. Did you ever have a fire in your home? What did you do? What was the damage?
5. Did you ever have an accident at home? What happened?
6. Did your home ever have water damage? What caused it? What did you do about it?
7. Were you ever bitten by a dog? What did you do?
8. Do you have insurance? What kind? What does it cover?
9. Do people in your native country or city carry insurance? What kind?

Group Activity: How Insurance Helps

Look at these pictures. Discuss what is happening. How can insurance help these people? Share your answers with the class.

You and Your Landlord

Partners' Interview: Your Landlord

Ask your partner these questions. Report your interview to the class.

1. Do you know your landlord (landlady)? What is his or her name?
2. Does your landlord live in the same house as you?
3. Does your landlord take good care of the building?
4. Did you ever have any problems with your landlord? What were they? What happened?
5. Does your community have a tenants' rights organization? What is its purpose?
6. When should you call the Department of Health?
7. Does your building have a superintendent? What does he do? Do you know him? Does he help you sometimes?
8. Is your building in good condition? Why or why not?

Class Discussion: Hazardous Conditions

Look at these two pictures. What is wrong? What is the danger? How would you get help to fix these problems in your apartment?

Group Problem Solving: Problems with Your Landlord

Read these situations. Decide on a solution. Report your solutions to the class.

1. The tenant can't pay his rent on time, but the landlord wants the money to pay utility bills.
2. The tenant wants to nail bookcase shelves to the living room walls. The landlord doesn't want nails in the walls.
3. The tenant hates the neighbors. He wants to break his lease and move. The landlord says no.
4. There is lead paint in the kitchen. It is peeling. The tenant wants the kitchen painted.
5. It's May 25 and it's cold. The landlord turned off the heat on May 15. The tenant wants the heat turned on.
6. The landlord is raising the rent again. He says taxes and utilities are more expensive. The tenant says he cannot pay more rent.
7. The stairs are broken. The tenant wants them fixed. The landlord says he cannot find a carpenter.

51

Utilities

Partners' Interview: Your Utilities

Ask your partner these questions. Report your interview to the class.

1. Do you pay for your *utilities* or does the landlord pay for them?
2. When does the meter reader come to read the *electric meter*? The *gas meter*?
3. Do you know how to read meters? Do you know where the meters are in your home?
4. How much per gallon does oil cost where you live? How is your home heated? How is the water heated in your home?
5. Do you ever have any problems with utilities? What do you do?
6. What happens if you don't pay your *utility bills*?

Class Discussion: Problems with Utilities

These people have problems with the utilities in their homes. What are the problems? How should they solve them? Did you ever have a similar problem? What did you do? Tell the class about it.

Fahrenheit and Centigrade

Class Activity: Making Conversions

Read this with your class.

In the United States, most temperatures are given in fahrenheit although centigrade is becoming more widely used.

To change centigrade to fahrenheit, multiply the centigrade reading by 9/5 and add 32.

When you know centigrade (celsius) (C°)	Multiply by 9/5 add 32	To get fahrenheit (F°)
20°C	20 × 9/5 = 36 + 32	= 68°F
10°C	10 × 9/5 = 18 + 32	= 50°F
0°C	0 × 9/5 = __ + 32	= __ F
37°C	__ × __ = __ + __	= ____

To change fahrenheit to centigrade, subtract 32, then multiply by 5/9.

When you know fahrenheit (F°)	Subtract 32, multiply by 5/9	To get centigrade (C°)
68°F	68 − 32 = 36 × 5/9	= 20°C
32°F	32 − 32 = __ × __	= __ C
212°F	__ − __ = __ × __	= __ C
80°F	__ − __ = __ × __	= ____

Partners' Problem Solving: Converting Centigrade →Fahrenheit, Fahrenheit → Centigrade

Solve these problems. Then compare answers with those of the rest of the class.

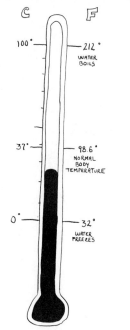

1. What is the centigrade temperature if the fahrenheit temperature is 99°? What kind of clothing would you wear?
2. What do you wear if the temperature is − 10°F?
3. If the temperature is 32°F, what is the centigrade temperature? Would you wear an overcoat?
4. If the temperature is 26°C, what is the fahrenheit temperature? What kind of clothes would you wear?
5. In summer in your native country or city, what are the average temperatures in fahrenheit? In centigrade?
6. In winter in the coldest part of your native country, what are the average temperatures in fahrenheit? In centigrade?
7. At what temperature fahrenheit does water boil? Centigrade?
8. What is normal body temperature fahrenheit? Centigrade?

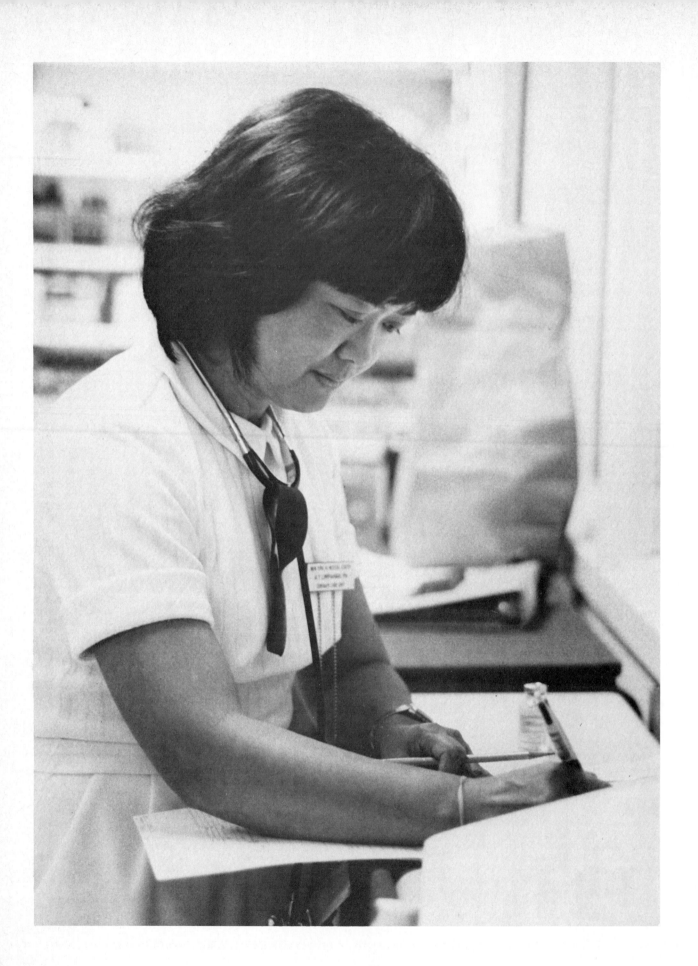

Employment

Childhood Ambitions

Group Activity: What Did You Want to Be?

Look at these pictures together. What work do these people do?

What did you want to be when you were a child? Did you fulfill your ambition? If you could be anything, what would you want to be? Fill in the last box. Share your answers with the group.

Report the results of your discussion to the class.

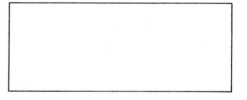

Your Occupation

Find Someone Who . . .

Find someone in the class who has done these jobs. Fill in as many as possible. Report your findings to the class. How many students have done each of these jobs?

_____
has worked in a factory.

_____
has worked in an office.

_____
has worked on a farm.

_____
has worked in a garage.

_____
has done housework.

Group Activity: What Is Your Job?

Fill in this chart with your group. Report your findings to the class.

Name	Job Title	Job Description

Group Interview: Students' Jobs

Each group should have one or more students who have a job (or who had a job in the past). Ask these questions. (This will prepare you for the next activity.)

1. Where do you work?
2. What is your job?
3. Do you work full-time or part-time?
4. What hours do you work?
5. Do you ever work overtime? Do you get paid more for overtime?
6. Do you like your job? How long have you been working there?
7. Did you work in your native country (city)? What job did you have?
8. Did you like your job? Would you like to have the same job in this country (city)?
9. Did you go to school to prepare for that job? What kind of school?
10. Will you have to go to school to prepare for the job you want in this country (city)? What will you have to study?

Speech: Your Job

After telling your group about your work, stand in front of the class and tell the whole class about your job. Include the information that you told your group. You may use notes, but do not read your speech. Speak slowly and clearly.

Speech and Audience Evaluations

Choose four students to evaluate each speech. Choose one student to evaluate the audience. Use the speech and audience evaluation forms in the Appendix on page 175.

Looking for a Job

Class Discussion: Finding a Job

Talk with the class about students' different experiences looking for jobs. Make a list on the board of possible ways to find a job.

Class Activity: Reading Want Ads

Read the employment opportunities in this classified section with your class. Discuss the abbreviations.

Community Activity: Looking for Want Ads

Bring the classified section of your local newspaper to class. Find a job that looks interesting. Read the ad to the class.

Partners' Role Play: Applying for a Job

Pick out a job to apply for. With your partner, role play a conversation with the personnel assistant to set up an appointment for a job interview.

Class Discussion: Wages

With your class, discuss the wages for the jobs in this classified section. What is the minimum wage where you live? What are benefits? Which is more important to you: high wages or good benefits? Why?

Employment

WAITRESSES/M Experienced, P/T, Mon-Fri, Call Between 9am-12.
555-0133

WAITRESS-m/f
For Dining Rm & Cocktail. Full/part time. Call 555-4400

Waitress M/F, bus help. Waitress for lunch only, bus help Ask for Lisa. Call after 2pm.
555-1234

WAITRESS/WAITER
experience required. All hrs. available.
Call 555-7973

WAREHOUSE General receiving, stock, pick/pack. Exp. preferred. Benefits. 555-9915

WAREHOUSE TRAINEE
General warehouse duties. Must be dependable. Permanent position.
555-6900

WAREHOUSEPERSON
Growing Electronics firm looking for person familiar w/basic warehousing functions. Clean drivers license.
Call for appointment: 555-0050

WAREHOUSE PERSON
MATURE, STEADY, PERMANENT
555-6947

★WAREHOUSE PERSONNEL★
F/T & P/T, Freight handling, layout orders, order duties.
555-2075

WAREHOUSE PERSON
Inventory control, shipping, receiving, packing. Highly responsible job. Benefits. 555-4321 before 10 am.

WAREHOUSE PERSONNEL
Distributor of video accessories, offers excel full/part time opp'ties for light warehouse duties include order picking, packing & shipping. Competitive salary & excel benfits. Interested applicants should apply in person. Call for appointment.
555-8823

Employment

WEEKDAY NIGHTSHIFT
Mon-Fri, 12am-8am. Group Home for retarded/autistic children. Excel benefits, frequent raises, car & lic. req.
555-1500

WELDERS
Exp in Arc & Heliarc welding on light gage steel. Good working conditions, good co benefits. Call Sam Jones 555-1235.

★**WORD PROCESSING**★
Int'l Consulting firm with Headquarters in Middletown needs exp'd person min 1 yr in Word Processor. Non-smoker, good benefits. Salary open. Call Joe 555-8500

★RESERVATIONIST/TELEMKTING
Join the most innovative TV sales company around! If you have a neat appearance, speak well, are detail oriented and accurate, we can offer salary, bonus, commission and an excellent benefit package. Let's talk. Call after 9 am. Ask for Marty.
555-6000

RETAIL SALES
Full and part time. Mature, Experience required. Call 9—5. Ask for Tom.
555-9512

RETAIL SALES CLERK P/T
Retail sales in Computer Center. General office duties. Learn word processing & data entry. Pleasant phone personality.
Call Helga
555-9035

RETAIL SALES
Like To Sell? Love A Challenge?
We are Stereos
looking for enthusiastic, vivacious sales people with energy and desire to work in retail atmosphere. 15—25 hours per week with many opportunities for advancement in our expanding company. Excellent clerical position also available in Commercial Sales Department. Please call 535-4425 for interviews.

Employment

RETAIL SALES, full time position for Highlands boutique. Call 555-1054.

SALES/CASHIER & STOCK
Part & Full time, excellent Company benefits. Apply Ladies Department. Call 555-8880

YARD HELP
For trucking co. no exp. necessary.
555-0051

YARD MAN
M/F in a lumber yard. Exp only. Excel pay. 555-2934

Youth Group Leader needed for children ages 3—10. For information call 555-3500

RUSSELL'S

COOKS,

WAITERS/WAITRESSES,

HOST/HOSTESS

DISHWASHERS

Now accepting applications for the above positions. We are looking for highly motivated, dedicated people with good communication skills. If you are interested in a career with us, apply Monday through Thursday 2pm-4pm. Russell's, Main Street, Highlands.

SALLY'S NEW FANGLED
HAMBURGERS

Help wanted F/T P/T, Days & evenings. Apply in person
555-9000

29. Sales Help Wanted

ANTIQUE store looking for salesperson. Open 6 days.
Write to BOX M5093
c/o this newspaper.

59

Job Interviews

Group Activity: Dressing for a Job Interview

Make a list of the differences between these two job applicants. Share your list with the class.

On the Board: How to Make a Good Impression

Make a list on the board of things to do in a job interview to make a good impression.

Partners' Role Play: Job Interview

With your partner, role play a job interview. Pick a job from the classified section of the newspaper. Fill out the employment application on the next page. Use these interview questions as a guide. Begin by introducing yourselves and making small talk.

Questions for the Interviewer

1. Which job are you applying for?
2. What kind of experience do you have for the job?*
3. What kind of education do you have?*
4. Do you have any special skills?*
5. Why did you leave your last job?*
6. Will you be able to work full time? Overtime? Saturdays?
7. Are you a citizen? If not, do you have permission to work in the U.S.? What is your visa status?
8. Are you interested in the job?

*Refer to application.

Questions for the Interviewee

1. What are the hours?
2. Is the job full-time or part-time? Is there overtime?
3. Will there be on-the-job training? What would my duties be?
4. Is there opportunity to advance?
5. Do you mind if I continue to go to school to study?
6. What are the benefits?
7. Are there many layoffs?
8. When will I know if I have the job?

Employment Application

EMPLOYMENT APPLICATION

<table>
<tr><td rowspan="3">PERSONAL</td><td colspan="2">NAME:</td><td>SOCIAL
SECURITY NO.</td></tr>
<tr><td colspan="2">PRESENT ADDRESS:</td><td>TELEPHONE
NUMBER</td></tr>
<tr><td>(NUMBER)</td><td>(STREET)</td><td></td></tr>
</table>

(CITY)	(STATE)	(ZIP CODE)

<table>
<tr><td rowspan="5">EDUCATIONAL</td><td rowspan="2">NAMES OF SCHOOLS</td><td rowspan="2">CITY & STATE</td><td colspan="2">MONTH & YEAR</td><td colspan="2">Graduated</td><td rowspan="2">YEAR</td><td rowspan="2">DEGREE</td></tr>
<tr><td>From:</td><td>To:</td><td>Yes ☐</td><td>No ☐</td></tr>
<tr><td></td><td></td><td></td><td></td><td>☐</td><td>☐</td><td></td><td></td></tr>
<tr><td></td><td></td><td></td><td></td><td>☐</td><td>☐</td><td></td><td></td></tr>
<tr><td></td><td></td><td></td><td></td><td>☐</td><td>☐</td><td></td><td></td></tr>
<tr><td></td><td></td><td></td><td></td><td>☐</td><td>☐</td><td></td><td></td></tr>
</table>

Previous work experience and service in the U.S. Armed Forces. Account completely for the last five years.

<table>
<tr><td rowspan="9">WORK EXPERIENCE & MILITARY</td><td rowspan="2">NAME & ADDRESS OF
LAST EMPLOYER</td><td colspan="2" rowspan="2">DATES</td><td rowspan="2">KIND OF
BUSINESS</td><td rowspan="2">DUTIES</td><td rowspan="2">APPROX.
WEEKLY
SALARY</td><td rowspan="2">REASON
FOR
LEAVING</td></tr>
<tr></tr>
<tr><td>1</td><td>FROM:</td><td>19</td><td></td><td></td><td></td><td></td></tr>
<tr><td></td><td>TO:</td><td>19</td><td></td><td></td><td></td><td></td></tr>
<tr><td>2</td><td>FROM:</td><td>19</td><td></td><td></td><td></td><td></td></tr>
<tr><td></td><td>TO:</td><td>19</td><td></td><td></td><td></td><td></td></tr>
<tr><td>3</td><td>FROM:</td><td>19</td><td></td><td></td><td></td><td></td></tr>
<tr><td></td><td>TO:</td><td>19</td><td></td><td></td><td></td><td></td></tr>
<tr><td>4</td><td>FROM:</td><td>19</td><td></td><td></td><td></td><td></td></tr>
</table>

	TO:	19				

EMPLOYMENT DESIRED:

☐ Permanent   ☐ Temporary   ☐ Part-time   ☐ Summer

WORK PREFERRED_____

WHO SHOULD BE NOTIFIED IN CASE OF EMERGENCY?

NAME: TELEPHONE NO.

PLEASE READ BEFORE SIGNING:

I affirm that all information included on this application is true and correct. Any false information I have given can be considered sufficient cause for discharge. I authorize all former employers to answer questions in reference to this application.   Signature   Date

Working Conditions

Class Discussion: On Strike

The workers in this picket line are on strike for better working conditions and higher wages. Tell the class about labor unions in your native country. Are they large and powerful? Do members go on strike? What does the government do about strikes?

Group Problem Solving: Negotiating

You and a few other employees want some improvements in the company where you work. The company president says he is willing to negotiate some improvements, but you don't know what he is really willing to give you. You must decide which improvements are the most important for your group. Then you must try to persuade the president to agree to make these improvements.

1. Decide which three of the issues below are most important for your group. Add to the list if you wish. Decide why they are most important.
2. Role play a meeting with an "owner" from another group to negotiate an agreement. Present your role play to the class.

IMPROVEMENTS:

better food in the cafeteria
better transportation
more chances for promotion
better salaries
longer vacations
safer equipment

_____
_____
_____

Problems at Work

Group Activity: Behavior at Work

Make a list of things you should do on the job (examples: be on time, ask questions, dress neatly) and a list of things you shouldn't do (examples: leave early, take things home, be absent). Compare your list with the lists of other groups. Make a master list on the board and discuss each item.

Group Activity: Discrimination

Talk about this picture. Make up a story to go with the picture. Tell the story to the class.

Class Discussion: Problems at Work

Have you ever had any problems or misunderstandings at work? With your class, discuss what happened and how other students would handle the problem.

Partners' Role Play: Solving Problems

Choose one of these problems or use one of your own. Practice the role play with your partner. Then present your skit to the class.

1. Roles: Boss, employee
   Place: Shoe factory
   Situation: The boss tells the employee to change his position for the day and operate a new machine. The boss assumes the employee knows how to work the new machine, but the employee has never worked that machine.

2. Roles: Employee, cafeteria worker
   Place: Company cafeteria
   Situation: The employee tells the cafeteria worker what kind of sandwich he or she wants, but the worker doesn't understand.

3. Roles: Two employees from the same department who speak two different languages.
   Place: Office
   Situation: One employee likes to listen to the radio while working. The noise bothers the other employee.

4. Roles: _____
   Place: _____
   Situation: _____

Losing Your Job

On the Board: Losing a Job

Make a list on the board of reasons for losing a job. Has anyone in your class ever lost a job for any of these reasons? Tell the class about it.

Class Vocabulary Activity: Unemployment

With your class, find out the answers to these questions.

1. What is the difference between **being fired** and being **laid off**?
2. What does **notice** mean?
3. What is **severance pay**?
4. Who gives you notice and severance pay?
5. What is the name of the unemployment agency in your state?
6. How will your state unemployment office help you find a job?
7. Are there any **job training programs** in your area? Will they pay you to learn new job skills?
8. How long can you collect **unemployment benefits** in your state?
9. What is the **maximum amount payable** for unemployment benefits?

Filling Out Forms: Collecting Unemployment Insurance

To collect unemployment benefits, you have to fill out a declaration form in most states. Discuss the vocabulary on this form with your class.

COMMONWEALTH OF MASSACHUSETTS · DIVISION OF EMPLOYMENT SECURITY

Social Security Account Number

job insurance

WEEKLY BENEFIT STATEMENT

DO NOT WRITE IN THIS BLOCK

WARNING: ANSWER ALL QUESTIONS CAREFULLY. CLAIMS ARE INVESTIGATED. FALSE STATEMENTS CAN BRING A FINE OR JAIL OR BOTH.

1. DURING THE WEEK ENDING_____

a. Did you work either for an employer or in self-employment? .... YES ☐ NO ☐
   If "YES", enter earnings $_____ Name of employer _____

b. Did you look for work with anyone other than your last employer? .... YES ☐ NO ☐

c. Did you refuse any work? .... YES ☐ NO ☐

d. Did you attend any school or college? .... YES ☐ NO ☐

e. Did you receive, or have you applied for, any money for reasons below? ..... YES ☐ NO ☐
   (1) Severance, dismissal or retroactive pay (3) Bonus or Gratuity (5) Pension of Any Kind
   (2) Vacation pay (4) Workman's Compensation (6) Education or training allowance as a veteran

f. Were you able and willing to accept work on all **full time** shifts, customary for
   your occupation.. YES ☐ NO ☐

g. Did the number of your dependent children increase or decrease? .... YES ☐ NO ☐

2. DID YOU CHANGE ADDRESS SINCE YOU LAST REPORTED? .... YES ☐ NO ☐
   If "YES", enter new address_____

Zip Code

The above answers are given under the penalties of perjury.

Signature _____

IMPORTANT! (See Over)

Form 3099 Rev. 1-80 3000M-5-80-152729

Banking

Class Discussion: Using a Bank

Discuss these questions with your class.

1. Do you have a bank account? What kind of account is it? Checking? Savings? Other?
2. How much interest does your bank give on a savings account?
3. Do you get a bank statement every month from your checking account? What does the statement include?
4. Who balances the checkbook in your family?
5. How do you cash checks?
6. Does your bank have an electronic teller? Do you ever use it? How do you use it?
7. What should you do if your paycheck is lost or stolen?
8. What happens if you overdraw your account (write checks for more money than is in your account)?

Partners' Vocabulary Exercise: Banking Terms

Discuss the vocabulary with your partner. Fill in the boxes together.

> personal loan
> home improvement loan
> safe deposit box
> Christmas club
> bank by mail envelope
> travelers checks

1.

A loan made by a bank or a loan company for your personal use. There is always an interest charge.

2.

A box in the bank where you can store anything valuable such as jewelry or papers. You pay a yearly fee for its use and receive a key to open the box.

3.

A savings account which usually begins around New Year's and terminates shortly before Christmas. You must deposit the same amount every week. Sometimes the interest is lower on this type of savings account.

4.

A postage-paid envelope in which you send deposits to your bank.

5. ☐☐☐☐☐☐☐☐☐ ☐☐☐☐☐

Certificates which may be used as money around the world. They are not **valid** until you sign them, and they are safer than cash. You buy them for a small fee at the bank.

6. ☐☐☐☐ ☐☐☐☐☐☐☐☐☐☐ ☐☐☐☐

A loan made by a bank or loan company specifically for use in improving your home (a new room, a new roof, a garage, etc.).

Class Activity: Depositing Money

*When you deposit money in a savings account or a checking account, you must fill out a **deposit ticket**. Fill out this deposit ticket to put a check for $125.63 and $50.00 cash in your savings account. What is your total deposit? Write it on the deposit ticket.*

Name _____

Address _____

_____

DATE _____ 19____

DEPOSIT TICKET

CURRENCY		
COIN		
TOTAL CHECKS		
TOTAL		

A Z ⫶ 0 0 6 8 ⫶ 1

ACCOUNT NUMBER

Partners' Activity: Endorsing a Check

You must endorse a check (write your signature on the back of the check) before you deposit it. Do you know how to endorse a check to another person? Endorse this check to your partner.

67

Partners' Role Play: New Depositor at a Bank

Practice this role play with your partner. Then present it to the class.

Roles: Bank teller, new depositor
Place: Bank
Situation: A new depositor wants to deposit a check to his or her new account. The bank teller must explain what to do.

Partners' Activity: Checkbook

With your partner, look at this sample page from a checkbook. How much money is in the account now? (What is the balance?)

Who was paid on 6/4? (description of deposit) How much was paid? (amount of check)

How much money was put into the checking account on 6/4? (amount of deposit)

CHECK NO.	DATE	CHECKS ISSUED TO OR DESCRIPTION OF DEPOSIT	(−) AMOUNT OF CHECK	√ T	(−) CHECK FEE (IF ANY)	(+) AMOUNT OF DEPOSIT	BALANCE
		PLEASE BE SURE TO **DEDUCT** ANY PER CHECK CHARGES OR SERVICE CHARGES THAT MAY APPLY TO YOUR ACCOUNT					223 00
411	6/4	TO/FOR Dr. G. Katz	17 50				17 50 / 205 50
	6/4	TO/FOR deposit				63 00	63 — / 268 50
		TO/FOR					
		TO/FOR					
		TO/FOR					
		TO/FOR					

Class Activity: Writing Checks

Fill in this check to a utility company, a store, or a charity. Sign it. Then record it in the checkbook above. Subtract the amount from the balance. What is the new balance? Tell the class what you wrote.

No. _____	
_____ 19 ____	53 - 88 / 113
PAY TO THE ORDER OF _____ $ _____	
_____ DOLLARS	
essexbank	
ESSEX COUNTY, MASSACHUSETTS	

Class Discussion: Bank Accounts

What are the advantages and disadvantages of having a checking account? A savings account?

Taxes

Class Vocabulary Activity: Kinds of Taxes

Read this information and discuss the vocabulary.

In the United States, federal income taxes are due on April 15 every year. Many people fill out the **forms** themselves; others hire **accountants** to fill out the **forms** for them.

There are also **state taxes** and **city taxes**. In many areas, people pay **sales tax** on certain items, **property tax** on real estate, and **excise tax** on cars.

Class Discussion: Tax Deadlines

Sometimes people wait until the last minute to fill out their tax forms. This man waited until the *deadline*. How do you know that? What problems do you think he is having? Is it good or bad to wait until the last minute?

Class Discussion: Your Taxes

Find out the answers to these questions.

1. Does your city or state have a sales tax? What is it? What items are taxed? What do the tax revenues pay for?
2. What other state and local taxes are there? What are they for? What percentage are they?
3. Do you pay federal income tax? What percentage of your gross income is it?
4. What is a tax loophole? Who benefits most from loopholes?
5. Are taxes going up or down? Why? What good things come from tax money?
6. Are taxes the same in your native country and the United States? If not, how are they different?

69

Group Problem Solving: Imposing Taxes

Choose one of these problems to discuss with your group. Decide on a course of action and report your decision to the class.

1. You are members of the City Council. Your city is facing a fiscal crisis: there is not enough money to pay for city services. You have five choices:
   1. Lay off one-quarter of the police force.
   2. Lay off one-half of the fire department.
   3. Lay off one-fifth of the teachers and close two schools.
   4. Eliminate trash collection.
   5. Raise property taxes.

2. You are members of your town's Board of Selectmen. Your town has grown very fast and the old sewage system is inadequate. People are complaining about the health hazard. You must find a way to raise money for a modern sewage treatment system. Will you raise property taxes? Create a new tax for users? Create a one-time charge? Do you have other ideas?

3. You are members of the U.S. House of Representatives in Washington, D.C. It is an election year. The President of the United States has proposed a tax plan that will reduce taxes and increase defense spending. The voters in your state want more federal aid and less defense spending this year. What will you do and how will you vote on the President's tax plan?

Social Security

Class Reading Activity: Getting a Social Security Card and Benefits

Read this information with your class. Discuss the vocabulary.

Social Security provides you and your family with continuing income when your earnings stop or are reduced because of retirement, disability, or death. The Social Security deduction on each paycheck goes into your fund for this purpose.

Write or call the Social Security office:

1. when you cannot work because of illness or injury that will last one year or more.
2. when you are 62 or older and want to retire.
3. when you are almost 65 and don't want to retire. (You may receive Medicare benefits even if you don't retire at 65.)
4. when someone dies in your family who has been working.
5. when you, your wife or husband, or your dependent children suffer permanent kidney failure.

It is important for you to call, visit, or write any Social Security office before you reach 65, not only about retirement checks but also about Medicare, which is available whether or not you retire. Medicare is hospital insurance and medical insurance to help protect people 65 and over from the high costs of health care. Disabled people under 65 who have been entitled to Social Security disability benefits for 24 or more months are also eligible for Medicare. Insured workers and their dependents who need dialysis treatment or a kidney transplant because of permanent kidney failure also have Medicare protection.

Class Discussion: Social Security

Answer these questions with your class.

1. What is the current percent of F.I.C.A. (Social Security) deductions for employees?
2. Do you know anyone who has received Social Security benefits? What were they?
3. Is there a social security system in your native country? What benefits does it provide? How is it paid for?

Poll the Class: Opinions about Social Security

Take a poll of your class. Write the results on the board. What do you think?

	Yes	No	No Opinion
The present U.S. Social Security system is good.			
Social Security should include nationalized health care for everyone.			
The Social Security system in my native country is better than the U.S. system.			
Social security should not be mandatory.			

5

Transportation and Travel

Commuting

Partners' Interview: Your Commuting

Ask your partner these questions. Present your interview to the class.

1. How do you come to school?
2. How far do you live from school?
3. How long does it take you to get to school?
4. If you work, how do you get there? How far do you travel?
5. How long does it take you to get to work?

Find Someone Who . . .

Find someone in your class who uses each type of transporation.

_____
has taken a train to school.

_____
has taken a bus to school.

_____
has gone to school in a car-pool.

_____
has walked to school.

_____
has taken a subway to school.

Other: _____
_____

Poll the Class: Student Transportation

Take a poll of your class. Fill in this chart together.

STUDENT TRANSPORTATION TO SCHOOL	
Transportation	**Number of Students**
bus	
carpool	
train	
subway	
walk	
Other: _____	

Partners' Activity: Stuck in Traffic

What is happening in this strip story? With your partner, make captions for each frame. Compare your captions with those of other students.

_____

_____

_____

Class Discussion: Traffic

Do you ever have trouble with traffic? What do you do to avoid traffic?

When is traffic the worst where you live?

Partners' Activity: Your Route to School

Make a map to show how to get from school to your house. Include street names and landmarks. Explain your map to your partner.

Public Transportation

Community Activity: Survey of Public Transportation

Find someone outside your class who has used public transportation. Ask these questions and write the responses. Report your interview to the class. What does the class survey show about attitudes toward public transportation?

Survey Questions
1. Do you ever ride the subway (bus, train)?
2. Where do you go?
3. What stop do you get on?
4. Is it close to your home?
5. How long does the ride take?
6. What stop do you get off?
7. What is the fare?
8. Is the subway (bus, train) clean or dirty?
9. Is it safe? Is it safe at night? Why or why not?
10. Do you read on the way? If so, what do you read?
11. Is it crowded when you travel?
12. What problems have you had with public transportation?
13. Do you like public transportation? Why or why not?

Partners' Activity: Reading Train Schedules

Read the train schedule with your partner to find out the answers to these questions. Compare your answers with the rest of the class.

1. If you have to be in New York at 8:00 A.M., what train must you take from Port Washington?

2. If you're going to Flushing for an appointment at 11:30 A.M., what train must you take from Plandome?

3. If you're going to the museum in New York on a Sunday and you have to meet your friend at noon, what train do you take from Manhasset?

4. If you live in New York and are going to a dinner party in Port Washington on Saturday night at 8:00, what train should you catch?

5. When are the off-peak hours during the week, coming to and going from New York?

6. How many smoking cars are in a 10-car train? What is the location?

TO WOODSIDE AND NEW YORK
MONDAY TO FRIDAY, EXCEPT HOLIDAYS

Leave			Arrive		
Port Wash.	Plandome	Manhasset	Flushing	Woodside	New York
AM	AM	AM	AM	AM	AM
12:39	12:44	12:46	1:05	1:13	1:23
1:39	1:44	1:46	2:05	2:12	2:23
3:39	3:44	3:46	4:05	4:12	4:22
5:09	5:14	5:16	5:36	5:42	5:52
5:39	5:44	5:46	6:05	6:11	6:21
6:22	6:27	6:29	6:49	6:57	7:08
6:42	6:47	6:49	7:06	....	7:26
6:58	7:03	7:06	....	....	7:32
....	7:33	7:36	....	....	8:03
7:36	7:41	7:44	....	....	8:10
7:47	7:52	7:55	8:12	8:18	8:29
8:06	8:11	8:14	....	....	8:40
8:17	8:22	8:25	....	....	8:56
8:41	8:46	8:49	....	....	9:15
9:08	9:13	9:16	....	9:32	9:43
9:35	9:40	9:42	9:57	10:05	10:15
10:05	10:10	10:12	10:29	10:36	10:46
10:35	10:40	10:42	10:58	11:07	11:17
11:05	11:10	11:12	11:29	11:37	11:47
11:35	11:40	11:42	11:58	12:07	12:17
12:05	12:10	12:12	12:29	12:37	12:47
12:35	12:40	12:42	12:57	1:05	1:15
1:05	1:10	1:12	1:29	1:37	1:47
1:35	1:40	1:42	1:57	2:05	2:15
2:05	2:10	2:12	2:29	2:37	2:47
2:35	2:40	2:42	2:57	3:05	3:15
3:05	3:10	3:12	3:29	3:37	3:47
3:35	3:40	3:42	3:58	4:07	4:17
4:05	4:10	4:12	4:28	4:34	4:44
4:35	4:40	4:42	5:02	5:10	5:22
5:00	....	....	5:18	5:25	5:40
5:23	5:28	5:30	....	5:47	5:58
6:23	....	....	6:29	6:41	6:48	6:58
7:09	7:14	7:16	7:35	7:42	7:53
7:39	7:44	7:46	8:05	8:12	8:23
8:09	8:14	8:16	8:35	8:42	8:53
8:39	8:44	8:46	9:05	9:12	9:23
9:09	9:14	9:16	9:35	9:42	9:53
9:39	9:44	9:46	10:05	10:12	10:23
10:09	10:14	10:16	10:35	10:42	10:53
10:39	10:44	10:46	11:05	11:12	11:23
11:39	11:44	11:46	12:05	12:13	12:24
PM	PM	PM	AM	AM	AM

SATURDAY, SUNDAY & HOLIDAYS

Port Wash.	Plandome	Manhasset	Flushing	Woodside	New York
AM	AM	AM	AM	AM	AM
12:39	12:44	12:46	1:05	1:12	1:21
1:39	1:44	1:46	2:05	2:12	2:21
3:39	3:44	3:46	4:05	4:11	4:21
5:39	5:44	5:46	6:05	6:12	6:21
6:39	6:44	6:46	7:05	7:12	7:21
7:39	7:44	7:46	8:05	8:12	8:21
8:39	8:44	8:46	9:05	9:12	9:21
9:09	9:14	9:16	9:35	9:42	9:51
9:39	9:44	9:46	10:05	10:12	10:21
10:39	10:44	10:46	11:05	11:12	11:21
11:39	11:44	11:46	12:05	12:12	12:21
12:09	12:14	12:16	12:35	12:42	12:51
12:39	12:44	12:46	1:05	1:12	1:21
1:09	1:14	1:16	1:35	1:42	1:51
1:39	1:44	1:46	2:05	2:12	2:21
2:09	2:14	2:16	2:35	2:42	2:51
2:39	2:44	2:46	3:05	3:12	3:21
3:39	3:44	3:46	4:05	4:12	4:21
4:39	4:44	4:46	5:05	5:12	5:21
5:39	5:44	5:46	6:05	6:12	6:21
6:39	6:44	6:46	7:05	7:12	7:21
7:09	7:14	7:16	7:35	7:42	7:51
7:39	7:44	7:46	8:05	8:12	8:21
8:09	8:14	8:16	8:35	8:42	8:51
8:39	8:44	8:46	9:05	9:12	9:21
9:39	9:44	9:46	10:05	10:12	10:21
10:39	10:44	10:46	11:05	11:12	11:21
11:39	11:44	11:46	12:05	12:12	12:21
PM	PM	PM	AM	AM	AM

FROM NEW YORK AND WOODSIDE
MONDAY TO FRIDAY, EXCEPT HOLIDAYS

Leave			Arrive		
New York	Woodside	Flushing	Manhasset	Plandome	Port Wash.
AM	AM	AM	AM	AM	AM
12:20	12:30	12:37	12:57	12:59	1:04
1:20	1:30	1:37	1:57	1:59	2:04
3:20	3:30	3:37	3:57	3:59	4:04
5:30	5:40	5:47	6:06	6:08	6:13
6:39	6:49	6:56	7:15	....	7:20
8:00	8:00	8:08	8:29	8:31	8:36
8:20	8:30	8:37	8:57	8:59	9:04
8:50	9:00	9:06	9:22	9:24	9:29
9:20	9:30	9:37	9:54	9:56	10:01
9:50	10:00	10:06	10:22	10:24	10:29
10:20	10:30	10:37	10:54	10:56	11:01
10:50	11:00	11:06	11:22	11:24	11:29
11:20	11:30	11:37	11:54	11:56	12:01
11:50	12:00	12:06	12:22	12:24	12:29
12:20	12:30	12:37	12:54	12:56	1:01
12:50	1:00	1:06	1:22	1:24	1:29
1:20	1:30	1:37	1:54	1:56	2:01
1:50	2:00	2:06	2:22	2:24	2:29
2:20	2:30	2:37	2:54	2:56	3:01
2:50	3:00	3:06	3:22	3:24	3:29
3:20	3:30	3:37	3:54	3:56	4:01
3:50	4:00	4:06	4:22	4:24	4:29
4:22	———	———	4:48	4:51	4:56
4:47	———	———	5:14	5:16	5:21
5:03	———	———	5:37	5:39	5:44
5:11	———	———	5:40	———	5:49
5:25	———	———	5:52	5:54	6:01
5:43	———	———	6:11	6:14	6:20
6:20	6:30	6:37	6:57	6:59	7:04
6:50	7:00	7:07	7:27	7:29	7:34
7:20	7:30	7:37	7:57	7:59	8:04
7:50	8:00	8:07	8:27	8:29	8:34
8:20	8:30	8:37	8:57	8:59	9:04
8:50	9:00	9:07	9:27	9:29	9:34
9:20	9:30	9:37	9:57	9:59	10:04
9:50	10:00	10:07	10:27	10:29	10:34
10:20	10:30	10:37	10:57	10:59	11:04
10:50	11:00	11:07	11:27	11:29	11:34
11:20	11:30	11:37	11:57	11:59	12:04
11:50	12:00	12:07	12:27	12:29	12:34
PM	MID	AM	AM	AM	AM

SATURDAY, SUNDAY & HOLIDAYS

New York	Woodside	Flushing	Manhasset	Plandome	Port Wash.
AM	AM	AM	AM	AM	AM
12:20	12:30	12:37	12:56	12:58	1:03
1:20	1:30	1:37	1:57	2:00	2:05
3:20	3:30	3:37	3:57	4:00	4:05
5:20	5:30	5:37	5:57	6:00	6:05
6:20	6:30	6:37	6:57	7:00	7:05
7:20	7:30	7:37	7:57	8:00	8:05
7:50	8:00	8:07	8:27	8:30	8:35
8:20	8:30	8:37	8:57	9:00	9:05
9:20	9:30	9:37	9:57	10:00	10:05
10:20	10:30	10:37	10:57	11:00	11:05
10:50	11:00	11:07	11:27	11:30	11:35
11:20	11:30	11:37	11:57	12:00	12:05
11:50	12:00	12:07	12:27	12:30	12:35
12:20	12:30	12:37	12:57	1:00	1:05
12:50	1:00	1:07	1:27	1:30	1:35
1:20	1:30	1:37	1:57	2:00	2:05
2:20	2:30	2:37	2:57	3:00	3:05
3:20	3:30	3:37	3:57	4:00	4:05
4:20	4:30	4:37	4:57	5:00	5:05
5:20	5:30	5:37	5:57	6:00	6:05
5:50	6:00	6:07	6:27	6:30	6:35
6:20	6:30	6:37	6:57	7:00	7:05
6:50	7:00	7:07	7:27	7:30	7:35
7:20	7:30	7:37	7:57	8:00	8:05
8:20	8:30	8:37	8:57	9:00	9:05
9:20	9:30	9:37	9:57	10:00	10:05
10:20	10:30	10:37	10:57	11:00	11:05
11:20	11:30	11:37	11:57	12:00	12:05
PM	PM	PM	PM	MID	AM

PROBLEMS, COMPLAINTS 9am–5pm WEEKDAYS
PUBLIC AFFAIRS 1-718-526-6020
LOST & FOUND 1-718-526-0020 or 1-516-742-3900
MAIN SWBD. 1-718-990-7400 or 1-516-742-3900

REFERENCE NOTES
Light type–denotes AM trains.
Bold face type–denotes PM trains.
Shaded areas indicate trains not honoring off-peak tickets.
HOLIDAYS–New Year's Day, Washington's Birthday, Memorial Day, Independence Day, Labor Day, Thanksgiving and Christmas.

New Location of Smoking Cars in All Trains
4 Car
5 Car
6 Car
7 Car
8 Car
9 Car
10 Car
11 Car
12 Car
12th Car 11th Car 10th Car 9th Car 8th Car 7th Car 6th Car 5th Car 4th Car 3rd Car 2nd Car 1st Car
West End Of Train   *Bar Cart service if available   East End Of Train

Courtesy of L.I.R.R.

Community Activity: Your Local Schedules

Bring in local bus and train schedules from your community. Practice reading the schedules with your group. Do you read them the same way as this schedule? What stop do you get on? Where have you gone on the train?

Group Activity: Long Distance Travel by Bus

With your group, plan a bus trip from Cleveland, Ohio to Birmingham, Alabama. Answer the following questions. Compare your answers with those of the rest of the class.

1. What time does the bus leave Cleveland?
2. What time does it stop for a meal? In what city?
3. Where does the bus make a rest stop at 12:40?
4. How many package express service stops are there en route?
5. When does the bus arrive in Birmingham? Is it morning or evening?

SPECIAL SYMBOLS

f — Flag stop. Bus will stop on signal to receive and discharge passengers.

■ — Rest stop.

✕ — Meal or lunch stop.

HS — Highway stop — does not go into town or agency.

D — Stops only to discharge passengers at agency or in town.

(LB) — Lock box for deposit of express during station closed hours.

🚌 — Package express pickup and delivery service available.

⊕ — Change buses.

ss — Station stop.

x — By connection.

△ — Rest or meal stop before arriving station.

△ — Rest or meal stop after leaving station.

AM — Light face figures.

PM — Bold face figures.

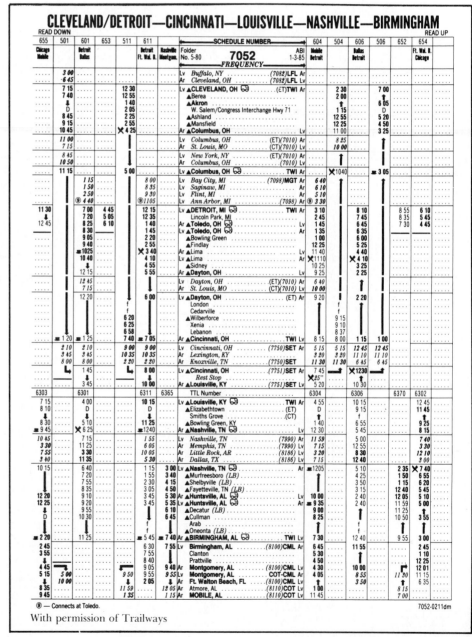

With permission of Trailways

78

Cars

Partners' Activity: Comparing Cars

With your partner, decide who will look at this picture and who will look at the car picture in the Appendix (page 176). DO NOT LOOK AT BOTH PICTURES! Partner A describes the picture on this page, then Partner B describes the car on page 176. With your partner, make a list of the differences. Compare your list with those of the rest of the class.

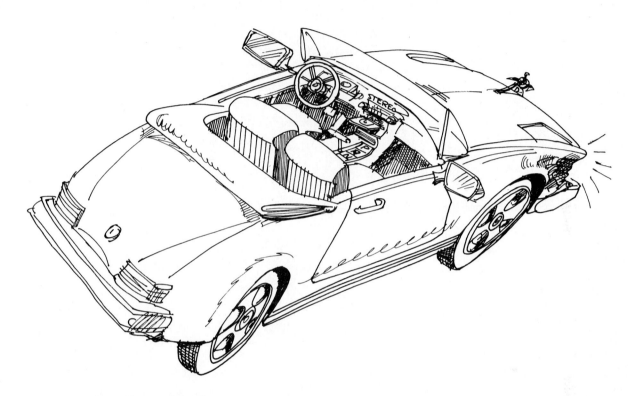

Class Discussion: Favorite Cars

Make a list on the board of everyone's favorite kind of car. Discuss advantages of different kinds of cars.

Partners' Interview: Cars and Personality

Ask your partner these questions. What do the answers tell you about your partner's personality and goals in life?

1. What kind of car would you like to drive?
2. Describe it (or draw it).
3. How does this describe your personality?
4. What type of car would you least like to drive?
5. Describe it.
6. Why don't you like it?
7. What type of car would you most likely buy?
8. Describe it.
9. Why would you buy it? (financial consideration, family, etc.)
10. Is the kind of car you drive important to you? Why?

Group Discussion: Cars

Choose a note taker for your group to take notes on your discussion and to read the notes to the whole class afterwards.

1. Do you have a car?
   - What kind of car is it?
   - Where did you buy it?
   - When did you buy it?
   - Did you buy it new or used?
   - Is it an automatic or standard transmission?

2. Is it better to buy a car new or used? Why?

3. Does a car cost more in the United States than in your native country? How much does a car cost in your native country? In the United States?

4. Are there many highways where you live? Are they toll roads or freeways?

5. Are there speed limits in your native country? What are they? What happens if you go beyond the limit?

Other Vehicles

Group Activity: Different Vehicles

Write the names of these vehicles under each picture. Answer the questions with your group. Report your answers to the class.

1. Do many people ride bicycles or motorcycles in your native country?
2. Do motorcyclists wear helmets? Do you think it is a good idea to wear helmets?
3. Are motorcycles and bicycles expensive or cheap in your native country?
4. How do most people travel in your native country (or city)?
5. How do most people travel where you live now?
6. Have you ever driven a van? Where? What kind of van?
7. Have you ever driven a truck? How big was it? What did you carry in it? Where did you drive it?
8. Which of these vehicles do you need a license for?

On the Board: Students' Transportation

Make a list on the board of all the different kinds of vehicles that students in your class have driven or ridden in. Make another list of all the different kinds of animals that anyone in your class has ever ridden on. What is the most common kind of transportation in your class?

Driving

Filling Out Forms: Driver's License

Fill out this application. Is it similar to the application where you live? Discuss the vocabulary.

APPLICATION FOR DRIVER LICENSE

1 Last Name   First   Middle Initial

Name

2 Date of Birth   Month   Day   Year   Sex   **Proof Submitted**
                                           M   F

Birth/Sex

3 If you are presently a licensed New York driver, enter the motorist identification number exactly as it appears on your license.

MI

4 Number and Street (Mailing Address including Rural Delivery, Box No. and/or Apt. No.)

Street

5 City or Town   State

City/State

6 Zip Code   County of Residence

Zip   **County**

7 Has your address changed since your last license was issued?   ☐ Yes   ☐ No

8 Legal Address if different from Mailing Address

9 Height   **Restriction(s)**

10 Eye Color

Class Discussion: Your Driver's License

Discuss these questions with your class.

1. What tests do you have to pass to get a driver's license? Have you taken them? Did you pass them the first time?
2. What is a learner's permit? How can you get one?
3. What is the name of the state bureau that handles drivers' licenses where you live now? Where is it located?
4. What else does that bureau handle?

Partners' Role Play: Speeding

With your class, describe what is happening in this strip story. Then role play the situation with a partner.

Class Discussion: Speeding Ticket

Did you ever get a speeding ticket? Tell the class about it. How fast do you usually drive? Why?

Taking Care of Your Car

Partners' Activity: Flat Tire

With your partner, describe what is happening in this strip story. Write a caption for each picture. Read your captions to the class.

Did you ever have a flat tire? What did you do? Tell your story to the class.

Class Discussion: Taking Care of Your Car

Discuss these questions with your class

1. Where do you buy gas? What kind of gas does your car use? How much does gas cost? Do you pay cash or use a charge card?
2. Where do you buy oil for your car? How much oil do you put in the car? How much does a quart of oil cost? How often do you change the oil in your car?
3. Do you have to get your car inspected? When? How much does it cost? Where do you have your car inspected?
4. Where is the best place to buy tires? What kind of tires do you buy? Did you ever buy snow tires? Why do drivers use snow tires?
5. Do you buy antifreeze? When do you use it? Where do you put it?

On the Board: Servicing for Your Car

Make a list on the board of the things a mechanic should check when you take your car in to be serviced. Bring the list the next time you take your car to the service station.

Financing a Car

Group Activity: Buying a Car

(For this activity, bring in ads for new and used cars from the newspaper.)

Your group wants to buy a car.

Decide: 1. which car/which model (and why)
         2. new or used (and why)

Prepare: 1. a list of questions to ask the owner or dealer
         2. a list of things to look for when you go to see the car

Figure out how to finance
  1 cash or loan? (pros and cons)
  2 what is the current interest rate?
  3 can you get a loan? credit?
  4 what would your down payment be?
    your monthly payment?

Present your decision to the class and explain your reasons.

Filling out forms: Car Loan Application

Fill out this application. Discuss the vocabulary with the class.

Name_____

Address_____

_____

Phone Number_____

Age _____ Number of dependents_____

Bank _____

Real estate owned_____ Value_____ Mortgage_____

Driver's license number _____

Present employer_____

Business address _____

_____

Salary_____ How long employed there?_____

Previous car bought from_____

Credit references_____

List any loans you currently have:

Name	Address	Balance	Installments
1.			
2.			
3.			

Other references

Name	Address	Balance	Relationship
1.			
2.			

Date_____   Signature _____

Partners' Problem Solving: Simple versus Compound Interest

Solve this problem with your partner. Compare your answers with those of the rest of the class.

Situation:

You want to buy a used car. The car costs $3000. You have $600. You decide to borrow the rest of the money from a bank or a loan company. You will take three years to repay the loan. Bank A will lend you the money at 15% compound interest. Loan Company B will lend you the money at 12% simple interest. Which do you choose?

Compound interest: The interest you pay changes every year because you pay interest only on the amount (*principal*) you still owe.
Simple interest: The interest remains the same because you pay interest on the original principal.

Bank A: 15% compound interest

Year	Unpaid principal	Interest (15% of principal)		Principal paid	=	Total (interest + principal paid)
1	$2400	$360	+	$800	=	$1160
2	$1600	$240	+	$800	=	$1040
3	$ 800	$120	+	$800	=	$ 920
	Totals:					

Loan Company B: 12% simple interest

Year	Unpaid principal	Interest (12% of $2400)	+	Principal paid	=	Total (interest + principal paid)
1	$2400	$288	+	$800	=	$1088
2	$1600	$288	+	$800	=	$1088
3	$800	$288	+	$800	=	$1088
	Totals:					

Questions

1. What are the totals for each loan?
2. What does Bank A charge for a $2400 loan?
3. What does Loan Company B charge for a $2400 loan?
4. Which loan should you take? Why?

Insurance and Accidents

Class Vocabulary Activity: Your Insurance

Answer these questions with your class and discuss the vocabulary.

1. Do you have insurance for your car? What kind is it?
2. Does your state have **compulsory** (mandatory) **coverage**? What is **mandatory**? What is **optional**?
3. Do you have **comprehensive coverage**?
4. Do you understand your insurance policy? Bring it to class. Does it cover:
   - **theft**?
   - **fire**?
   - **collision**?
   - **broken windshield/glass**?
   - **explosions**?
5. What is the **deductible** on accidents?
6. What is your **liability**?

Class Discussion: Car Accidents

Was anyone in the class ever in a car accident? Tell the class about it.

Group Activity: Running a Stop Sign

With your group, describe this accident. Write a caption for each picture. Read your captions to the class.

_____ _____ _____
_____ _____ _____

Group Role Play: Fender Bender

A fender bender is a slight accident with no injuries. Plan a fender bender scene with your group, then present it to the class. Exchange this information with the other driver:

Car owner's name _____

Address _____

Insurance company _____

Name of person driving the car at the time of the accident (operator)

_____

Operator's address _____

Operator's license number _____

Car make _____ Type _____ Year _____

Write down details:

Time of accident _____

Road conditions _____

89

Traveling

Partners' Interview: Your Trip

Ask your partner these questions. Present your interview to the class.

1. What places have you visited in your native country?
2. Where have you traveled other than your native country (or city)?
3. Where have you traveled in the United States?
4. Tell about one trip you took:
   - How did you travel (by plane, bus, train, car)?
   - How long did the trip take?
   - Who did you go with?
   - Did you visit family or friends?
   - What did you do during the trip?
   - What did you enjoy most?
   - Would you like to return? Why?
5. Where would you like to visit? Why?

Speech: My Favorite Trip

Prepare a brief speech for your class about a trip you have taken. You may use note cards but do not read your speech. Illustrate your speech with photographs or postcards if possible. Use the speech and audience evaluation forms on page 175 of the Appendix.

Class Activity: Sightseeing

Make a list on the board of famous places in different parts of the world that tourists visit.

Take books out of the library and get brochures from travel agencies showing famous places for tourists. Bring them to class and look at them together.

Partners' Activity: Dream Trip

With a partner, plan a dream trip. Describe your trip to the class.

90

Group Discussion: Travel Accommodations

Discuss these questions with your group. Choose one student to report your discussion to the class.

1. When you take a trip, which accommodations do you prefer: Hotel? Motel? Tent? Other? Why?

2. Do you tip when you travel? How much do you think is appropriate to tip a bellhop? Room service? A taxi driver? A waitress? Is tipping customary in your native country? Tell the class about it.

3. Do you use traveler's checks when you travel? Why or why not?

Partners' Role Play: Getting Travel Information by Telephone

Choose one of these situations with your partner. Decide what questions to ask and write them down. Role play calling the appropriate place for information. Finally, demonstrate your phone call for the class.

1. You want to take a train to Los Angeles, California. Call Amtrak and ask about schedule and prices and how long the trip will take.
2. You want to buy a National Railroad pass for travel in Japan. Call your travel agent and ask for information.
3. You want information from an airline about a ticket to visit three cities in your native country. Decide where you want to go, what dates and time. Call for the information.
4. You want to make a round trip plane reservation to Chicago, Illinois. You want the cheapest rate possible.

Group Activity: Tips for Travelers

Choose one of these topics, then write a list of Tips for Travelers. Share your tips with the class.

1. What advice would you give to people who are planning to travel to your native country?
2. What advice would you give to people who are planning to come to the country (or city) you live in now?

Community Activity: Class Trip

Make a list on the board of all the places your class could go sightseeing. Bring in brochures and photographs and postcards if possible. Decide what trip to take. Choose a committee to make the arrangements. Have a good trip!

Travel in the United States

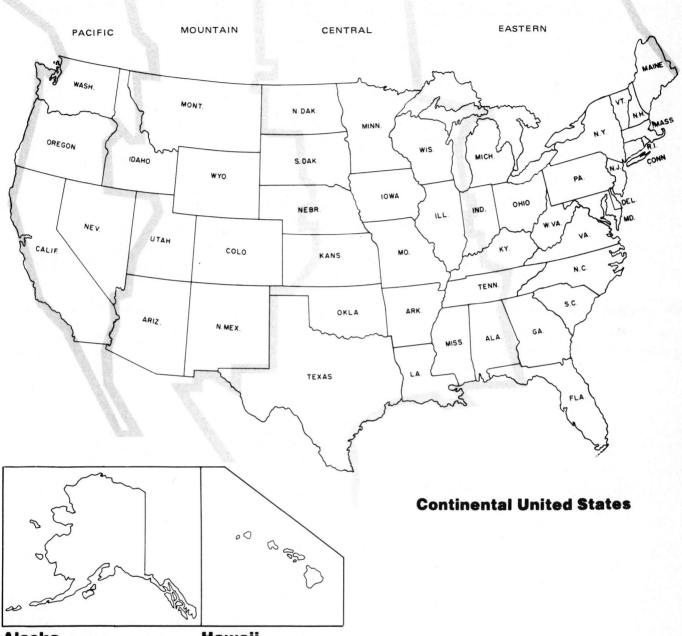

PACIFIC   MOUNTAIN   CENTRAL   EASTERN

Continental United States

Alaska   **Hawaii**

Partners' Activity: Crossing the U.S.A.

Answer these questions with your partner. Share your answers with the class.

1. When it is 9:00 A.M. in Boston, Massachusetts, what time is it in Phoenix, Arizona?
2. When it is noon in Olympia, Washington, what time is it in Chicago, Illinois?
3. What states would you cross driving from Florida to New York?
4. What states would you cross driving from Los Angeles, California, to Philadelphia, Pennsylvania? What time zones would you cross?
5. What states would you cross driving from Wisconsin to Texas?

Long Distance Travel

Group Discussion: Out of Water

Choose a note taker for your group to take notes on your discussion and to read the notes to the whole class afterwards.

1. What has happened to this traveler?
2. Where could he be?
3. How could he have avoided this problem?
4. What must he do now?
5. What precautions should you take when driving cross-country?

Class Activity: Geography Game

*One student begins by naming any city, state, or country. (**Student** #1: Germany) The next student must name another city , state, or country beginning with the last letter of the first student's choice (**y**). (**Student** #2: Yugoslavia: Student #3: Atlanta; etc.)*

Map Reading

Partners' Activity: Finding Your Way in New York

Partner A looks at the map in the Appendix (p. 171). Partner B looks at this map. Partner A gives the directions. Partner B draws the route on this map and writes the name of the destination in the correct place. When you have finished, compare your maps.

Do you want to visit New York City? Look at the map of part of Manhattan. Start at your hotel on Eighth Avenue and 42nd Street *(see*)* and find your way to the following places:

1. Times Square
2. Macy's Department store
3. Empire State Building
4. Public Library
5. Penn Station

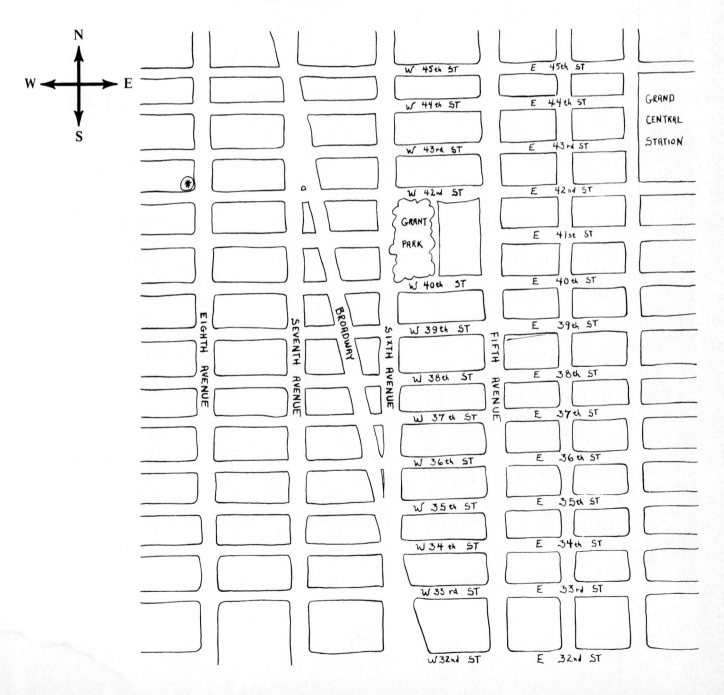

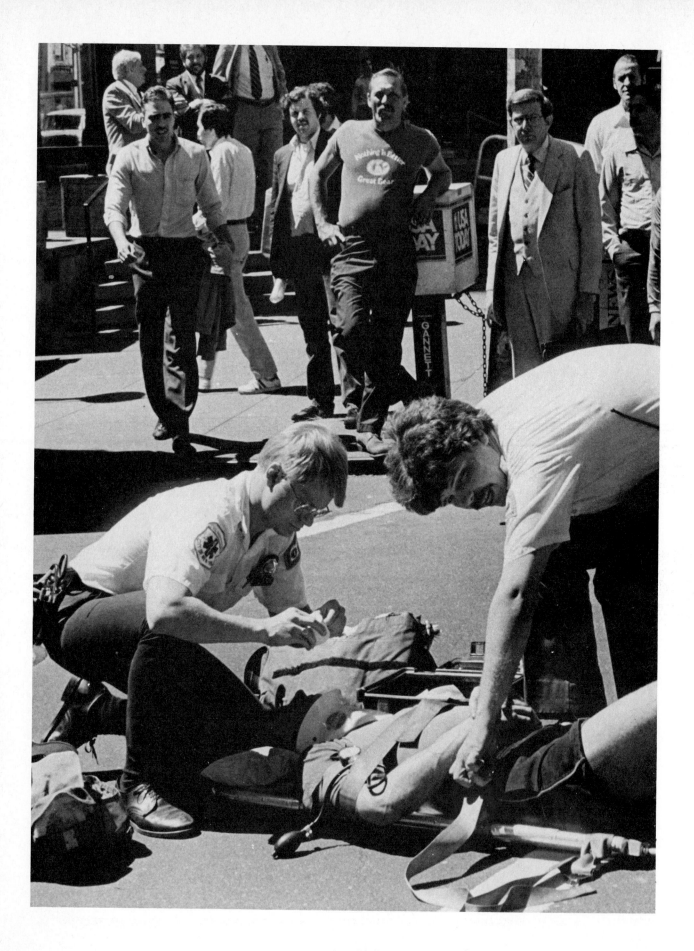

6

Health Care

A Healthy Diet

Group Discussion: Lunch

Choose a note taker for your group to take notes on your discussion and to read the notes to the whole class afterwards.

1. What are these two men eating for lunch?
2. Which lunch would you prefer?
3. Which lunch is more nutritious? Why?
4. Do you ever eat any food that isn't good for you? What kind?
5. Do people in your native country eat nutritious food for lunch? What do they eat?

Class Activity: Class Eating Habits

Fill in the two left-hand columns of this chart. Then, with your class, make a chart on the board. See how many answered YES and how many NO to each question. Copy the numbers on your chart.

	YOU		YOUR CLASS (Totals)	
	Yes	No	Yes	No
Eat a big breakfast				
Eat a big lunch				
Eat a big dinner				
Take vitamins				
Eat junk food				
Use prepared mixes				
Use frozen food				
Are on a diet				

Group Activity: Planning Meals

Label each food in the four food groups below. Add one more food to each group. Then plan three nutritious meals for one day: breakfast, lunch, and dinner. Make sure each meal is balanced. Share your menu with the class. Have the class vote on the best menu.

Meat group (protein, fat, vitamins)

  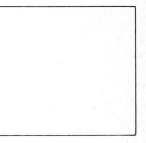

_____ _____ _____

Milk group (protein, fat, calcium, minerals, phosphorous, vitamins)

_____ _____ _____

Vegetable group (vitamins, carbohydrates, minerals)

_____ _____ _____

Bread-cereal group (carbohydrates, protein, vitamins, minerals)

_____ _____ _____

The Unhealthy Life

Group Activity: Bad Health Habits

Discuss these pictures with your group and write a caption for each picture. Compare your captions with those of the rest of the class.

The Human Body

Partners' Vocabulary Activity: Inside the Body

With your partner, fill in as many words as you can. Check the answers on page 173 of the Appendix. Practice pronouncing the vocabulary with the class.

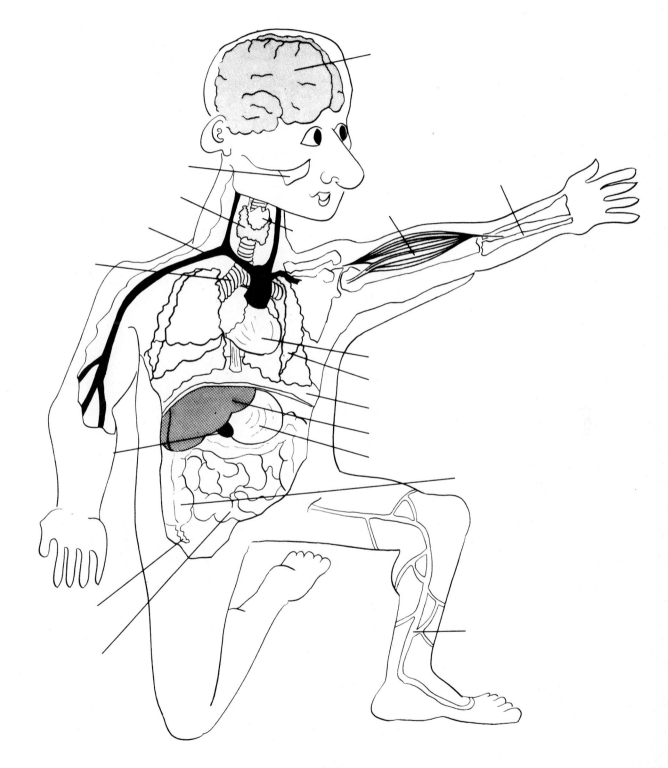

Health Problems

Group Activity: Common Health Problems

With your group, add to the list of medical problems below, and write the name of the part of the body where each of these problems occurs. Check your answers with the class. Has anyone in your group ever had any of these health problems? Tell the group about it.

1. Appendicitis   _____

2. Laryngitis   _____

3. Bronchitis   _____

4. Stroke   _____

5. Heart attack   _____

6. Hypothyroid (low thyroid)   _____

7. Cataracts   _____

8. Gallstones   _____

9. Kidney stones   _____

10. Jaundice   _____

11. Tuberculosis   _____

12. Ulcer   _____

13. Intestinal blockage   _____

14. Fracture (broken bone)   _____

15. Sprain   _____

16. _____   _____

17. _____   _____

Which Doctor?

Partners' Activity: Specialists

With a partner, add other specialists and health problems to the list. Then match the health problems with the correct specialist. Share your answers with those of the rest of the class.

PHYSICIANS	HEALTH PROBLEMS
General Practitioner	You have a heart condition.
Surgeon	You have a sick baby.
Cardiologist	You have a foot problem.
Orthopedist	You can't see well.
Obstetrician	You need a blood test.
Psychiatrist	You are pregnant.
Hematologist	You have a skin problem.
Ophthalmologist	You sneeze a lot.
Radiologist	You are sad and depressed.
Dermatologist	You break your arm.
Allergist	You need an X-ray.
Pediatrician	You don't feel well anymore.
Chiropodist	You have acute appendicitis.
_____	_____
_____	_____
_____	_____

Group Discussion: Your Doctor

Choose a note taker for your group to take notes on your discussion and to read the notes to the whole class afterwards.

1. Do you have a family doctor? What is his or her name?
2. When you go to the doctor, does a nurse assist the doctor? What does the nurse do?
3. Have you ever seen a specialist? What kind? Was the specialist able to help you?
4. Is choosing a doctor in your native country different from choosing a doctor in the United States? How?
5. Does your doctor make house calls? Do any doctors in your native country make house calls?
6. Look in the Yellow Pages of your local telephone directory under "Physicians" for a listing of your local doctors. Are there any other specialists listed besides the ones on the list above? Add them to the list.
7. Which do you prefer: doctors in your native country or doctors in the U.S.A.? Why?

Partners' Role Play: Making an Appointment with a Doctor

Role play making a doctor's appointment with a partner. Choose a doctor from the list. Write a telephone conversation in which a new patient makes an appointment to see the doctor about a problem. Practice your role play together, then present it to the class.

Roles: Patient, medical receptionist
Action: The patient asks for an appointment. The receptionist asks for information about the medical problem and the two decide on an appointment time.

Quick Cures

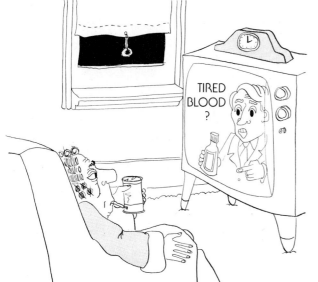 

Group Discussion: Miracle cures

Divide into four groups. Each group will discuss one picture. How do the people in these pictures believe they can solve their problems? What are they doing? How would you solve their problems? Report your discussion to the class.

Group Role Play: Helping a Friend with a Health Problem

Choose two students from your group to role play the situation in your picture. One student plays the person with the health problem. The other student plays a helpful friend.

Clinics

Class Activity: Clinic Services

In the United States, clinics provide public health care for everyone. Sometimes there is a small fee, but if you cannot afford to pay, it is free.

1. Write the name of the clinic under each picture. Use this list. Discuss with the class what each clinic is providing.

> Prenatal clinic
> Dental clinic
> Well-baby clinic
> V.D. clinic
> Immunization clinic
> Blood lead clinic

2. Does your community provide these services? Where?

3. Is there public health care in your native country? Is it good? Who visits the public health facilities? What services does the public health facility provide?

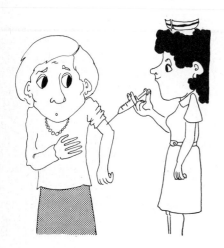

Dentists

Class Vocabulary Activity: What a Dentist Does

Read this with your class. Discuss the vocabulary and fill in the captions below.

A dentist cleans teeth, takes **X-rays** of teeth, fills **cavities**, and treats **gum diseases**. An **oral surgeon extracts** teeth and does other oral **surgery**. An **orthodontist** puts braces on teeth. A **dental assistant** helps the dentist.

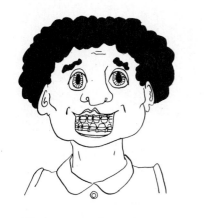

She's wearing braces. An _____ put them on.

He's having a tooth extracted. An _____ is extracting it.

She's having her teeth cleaned. A _____ and a _____ are cleaning them.

Partners' Interview: Your Teeth

Ask your partner these questions. Report your interview to the class.

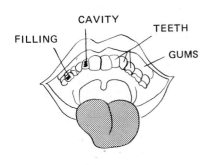

1. Have you ever had a toothache? What did you do about it?
2. Have you ever had your teeth cleaned at a dentist's office? How often? Do people in your native country have their teeth cleaned regularly?
3. Have you had any fillings? Did the drilling hurt? Do you prefer to have Novocain when you have a tooth filled?
4. Did you ever have a tooth extracted? Was it a wisdom tooth? Did you have Novocain? Gas? Sodium Pentothal?
5. Are there any differences between dental care in your native country and in the United States? Do people in your native country ever have gold fillings or gold caps put on their teeth?
6. How do you feel about going to the dentist? Do you ever avoid it?

Pharmacy

Group Activity: What to Buy In a Drugstore

What is happening in this picture? Make a list of everything your group has ever bought in a drugstore. Share your list with the class.

Partners' Role Play: Going to The Drugstore

Read the situations below and discuss the vocabulary. Add another situation to the list. Then choose one situation to role play. Present your role play to the class.

1. You need a nonprescription drug for a headache.
2. You need to refill an old prescription.
3. You want to buy a generic drug rather than a name brand.
4. _____

Medicine and First Aid

Group Activity: Your Medicine Chest

With your group, decide what each item is used for. What do you keep in your medicine chest at home?

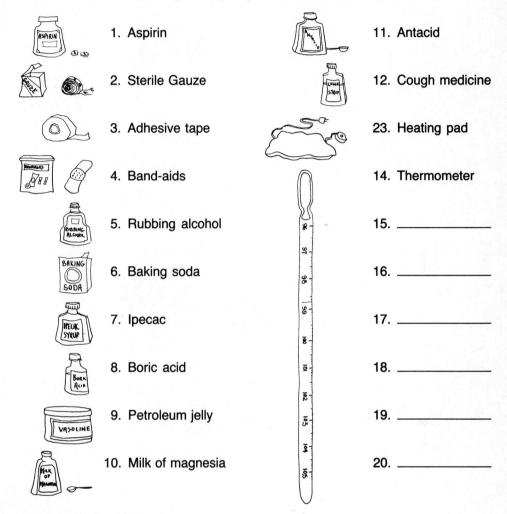

1. Aspirin
2. Sterile Gauze
3. Adhesive tape
4. Band-aids
5. Rubbing alcohol
6. Baking soda
7. Ipecac
8. Boric acid
9. Petroleum jelly
10. Milk of magnesia

11. Antacid
12. Cough medicine
23. Heating pad
14. Thermometer
15. _____
16. _____
17. _____
18. _____
19. _____
20. _____

On the Board: First Aid and Home Remedy List.

With your class, make a first aid and home remedy list on the board. Include everything you should have at home for emergencies or sickness.

Class Discussion: Home Remedies

Discuss these questions with your class.

1. What's the best way to cure the common cold? What remedies do you use? What do people in your native country or city do?
2. What's the best way to treat a stomach ache?
3. What do you do for a headache?

Class Activity: Medicine Labels

Bring in medicine bottles. Read the labels together.

Emergencies

Group Problem Solving: Emergency First Aid

Discuss these problems with your group. Report your solutions to the class.

Your neighbor is bitten by a stray dog.

A child takes too many aspirin tablets.

Your friend is bitten by a snake.

You stay in the sun too long.

Someone is stung by a bee.

You get a cinder in your eye.

Your friend has a nose-bleed.

Someone faints.

You get poison ivy.

Note: see p. 172 of the Appendix for answers.

Emergency Room

Group Discussion: In the Waiting Room

Discuss this picture. Decide why these people are in the Emergency Room. Then decide the following:

1. Which patient in this Emergency Room do you think should be treated first? Why?
2. Which should be treated second? Why?
3. Which could wait to be treated last? Why?

Make your choices as a group. Compare your choices with the rest of the class.

111

Class Discussion: Outpatient Clinic and Emergency Room

Discuss these questions with your class.

1. Has anyone in the class ever been taken to a hospital Emergency Room? Tell the class about it.

2. Has anyone ever gone to the Outpatient Clinic of a hospital? Was it for an emergency? Was it for something else? Tell the class about it.

3. How are hospital emergency rooms in your native country different from those in the United States?

Medical Decisions

Poll the Class: Organ Donors

Organ donors are people who donate organs from their bodies after they die. The organs are transplanted into another person. Common organ transplants are heart, kidney, and cornea. Find out how your class feels about organ transplants.

	Yes	No
I approve of organ transplants		
I would be willing to be an organ donor		
I would be willing to receive an organ transplant.		

Group Decision Making: Difficult Choices

Discuss these three situations with your group and decide what to do. Report your decisions to the class.

1. You are a group of doctors in a large hospital. A young woman was admitted to the hospital after a very serious car accident. She is in a coma and has serious, irreversible brain damage. She cannot breathe without an artificial respirator. With life support systems her heart will keep beating, but she will never wake up. If you do not attach life support systems, she will die. What should you do?

2. Your father is 80 years old and has been a patient in a nursing home for five years. He has many, serious physical problems and has already had surgery twice this year. The doctors say he needs surgery again. Without the operation, the doctors say he will die. Unfortunately, he has had a stroke, and cannot communicate his wishes to you. You must decide for him.

3. Your baby was born with a serious birth defect—an abnormal heart. He is six weeks old now, but the doctors say he will die soon unless his heart is replaced. They are willing to try a heart transplant as soon as a donor can be found. Will you authorize the operation?

Poisons

Class Discussion: Dangerous Substances

Discuss these questions with your class.

1. What is happening in this picture?
2. Where do you keep poisonous substances in your home? Do all the bottles and boxes have labels?
3. Is there a poison center in your city or town? What is the telephone number?
4. What should you say to the poison center if someone accidentally swallowed some bleach?
5. Ipecac will induce vomiting. You can buy it at the drugstore. How else can you induce vomiting?

Group Role Play: Calling for Help

Divide into small groups. Choose one of these poison emergencies to role play, or think of another one. Choose two students to role play an emergency telephone conversation for the class. Use the poison antidote chart on the next page to give the correct advice. Discuss the role play together to be sure the advice is clear.

1. Your toddler ate a bottle of baby aspirin.
2. The little boy you are baby-sitting for drank some lighter fluid.
3. You found your next-door neighbor unconscious, with an empty pill bottle lying next to her.
4. Your baby crawled under the sink and drank some insecticide.
5. _____

Antidote Chart

Poison	Antidote
Acids (CARBOLIC, hydrochloric, nitric, etc.)	Give milk of magnesia, chalk water, or baking soda solution. Then give milk. Keep the patient warm. Call the doctor or hospital.
Alkalies (LYE, caustic dye)	Give vinegar or lemon juice. Keep the patient warm. Call the doctor or hospital.
Kerosene (GASOLINE, wood alcohol, cleaning fluid, lighter fluid)	Do not induce vomiting. Call the hospital or your doctor.
Insecticide (There are usually antidotes on the package.)	Internal: Give milk, water, or salt water. Induce vomiting. Call the hospital or doctor. External: Remove and wash all clothing. Wash skin with soap and water.
Drug overdose (ASPIRIN, sleeping pills, etc.)	Call the hospital or doctor.
Unknown: Patient unconscious	Call an ambulance! Do not try to feed anything to an unconscious patient.

Class Vocabulary Activity: Labels

Read this label. List the new vocabulary on the board and discuss. Then discuss the questions with your class.

ROACH-OUT

KILLS INSECTS ON CONTACT

Reaches bugs through
cracks and crevices.

<u>Directions</u>: point valve toward direction of surface to be sprayed. Hold 8″ from surface. Spray upright until surface is saturated.

For ants: Apply around doors, windows, points of entry.

For cockroaches and waterbugs: Spray in cracks, crevices, baseboards, points of infestation.

Repeat as necessary.

<u>CAUTION</u>: Do not smoke when spraying.

Harmful if swallowed, inhaled or absorbed through skin.

Do not apply to humans, pets or dishes.

If swallowed contact a physician immediately.

Avoid contact with skin, eyes or clothing.

Wash hands thoroughly after use.

Contents under pressure. Do not place can on stove or radiator. Do not throw can into fire.

KEEP OUT OF REACH OF CHILDREN

---

1. For what kinds of bugs is this product useful?
2. How would you apply it if you had ants in your home?
3. Why does the label caution you against smoking when you use it?
4. Why should you wash your hands when you've finished?
5. What does **Repeat as necessary** mean?
6. What would you do if you accidentally sprayed some Roach-Out in your eyes?

Class Activity: Poisonous Substances

Bring in bottles or cans of poisonous substances you have in your home. Talk about the use of each. Why is it important to read the labels of these products?

Immunizations

Class Vocabulary Activity: Vaccinations

Read this with your class and discuss the vocabulary.

Vaccinations and innoculations give *immunity* to diseases. Doctors give babies *shots* to protect them against *German measles*, *mumps*, *tetanus*, *diphtheria*, *polio*, *typhoid*, and *measles*. Many older people get *flu* shots in the winter. Before people travel to some foreign countries, they get vaccinations for *cholera*. A *chest X-ray* or a *blood test* detects *tuberculosis*.

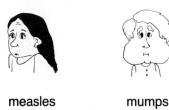

measles   mumps

Group Discussion: Your Immunizations

Choose a note taker for your group to take notes on your discussion and to read the notes to the whole group afterwards.

1. Have you ever had a chest X-ray?
2. Have you ever had a smallpox vaccination? Any other vaccination?
3. What vaccinations and innoculations do children in your native country have?
4. What vaccinations and shots do you have to have to travel to another country from your native country?
5. What childhood diseases are common in your native country? Which ones did you have?

Health Insurance

Partners' Vocabulary Activity: Insurance

See how many of these terms you know. Check your answers with the class.

comprehensive coverage
disability income
waiting period
premium
deductible

1. [ ] [ ] [ ] [ ] [ ] [ ] [ ] [ ] [ ] [ ]   [ ] [ ] [ ] [ ] [ ] [ ]

    Pays money after your sick pay is used up and you still need coverage.

2. [ ] [ ] [ ] [ ] [ ] [ ] [ ] [ ] [ ] [ ] [ ] [ ] [ ]   [ ] [ ] [ ] [ ] [ ] [ ] [ ] [ ]

    Includes hospital and out-of-hospital care.

3. [ ] [ ] [ ] [ ] [ ] [ ] [ ]   [ ] [ ] [ ] [ ] [ ] [ ]

    The time period after you apply for the insurance policy when you are *not* covered.

4. [ ] [ ] [ ] [ ] [ ] [ ] [ ]

    The amount you pay each month.

5. [ ] [ ] [ ] [ ] [ ] [ ] [ ] [ ] [ ] [ ]

    The amount the insurance doesn't cover.

Class Discussion: Your Policy

Discuss these questions with your class.

1. Are you covered by an insurance policy? Which company?
2. Is it an individual policy or a group policy?
3. Do you have an insurance card? When do you use it?
4. Do you have money deducted from your paycheck for insurance?
5. What benefits does your health insurance plan offer?
6. Why is it good to have health insurance?
7. Do people in your native country usually carry health insurance?
8. What is life insurance? Do you have any?
9. Why is it good to have life insurance?

7

Consumer Information

Saving Money on Food Shopping

Class Discussion: Shopping Hints

The pictures below illustrate ways of saving money on food shopping. Discuss each picture with your class.

Find Someone Who . . .

Find someone in your class who saves money on food shopping these ways. Add one more idea. Share your answers with the rest of the class. Which are the most popular ways of saving money on food shopping in your class?

1. _____

   plans shopping with advertised specials.

   What newspaper?

   _____

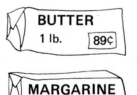

2. _____

   uses dry milk or evaporated milk.

   What brand?

   _____

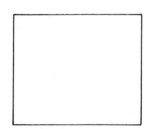

3. _____

   uses margarine instead of butter.

   Stick margarine or soft margarine?

   _____

4. Other:

Comparing Newspaper Ads

Partners' Activity: Comparison Shopping

When you read newspaper ads, you find out which items are the best buys each week. Compare the newspaper ads below and answer these questions. Share your answers with the rest of the class.

1. Where do you get the better buy for lean hamburger?
2. What fruits are the best buy this week?
3. What is the best way to buy chicken? At which store are the prices cheaper?
4. At which store do you get the better buy for apple juice?
5. At which store do you get the better buy for liquid detergent?
6. Is it cheaper to buy tomato sauce in a quart jar or a pint jar?
7. Is it cheaper to buy light cream in the half-pint size or the eighteen-ounce size?
8. Which is a better buy, peanut butter in the eighteen-ounce jar or in the forty-ounce jar?
9. Which is the better buy, rump roast or sirloin steak? Why?
10. At which store are most prices cheaper?

ACME MARKET

Chicken Parts	lb.	**$.79**
Sirloin Steak	lb.	**2.79**
Hamburg	lb. (lean)	**1.99**
Lettuce	head	**.89**
Cantaloupes	ea.	**1.29**
Apples	lb.	**.59**
Bananas	lb.	**.33**
Liquid Detergent	16 oz.	**1.79**
Tomato Sauce	1 qt. jar	**.89**
Beans	1 lb. can	**.45**
Peas	4 1 lb. can	**1.00**
Carrots	1 lb. can	**.35**
Apple Juice	½ gal.	**1.89**
Light Cream	½ pint	**.65**
Peanut Butter	18 oz. jar	**2.03**
Butter	1 lb.	**2.18**
Dry Milk	10 qts.	**2.99**

SAFEMART

Rump roast	lb.	**$2.95**
Hamburg	(lean) lb.	**1.39**
Chickens	(whole) lb.	**.69**
Apples	lb.	**.69**
Pears	6 for	**1.29**
SPECIAL Bananas	4 lbs./	**1.00**
Lettuce	2 for	**1.00**
Tomato sauce	1 pint jar	**.48**
Beans	(1 lb. can)	**.89**
Peas	(1 lb. can)	**.40**
Spinach	(1 lb. can)	**.45**
Apple juice	qt.	**.89**
Light cream	18 oz.	**1.50**
Peanut butter	40 oz. jar	**2.75**
Margarine	1 lb. box	**2/1.00**
Milk	gallon cont.	**1.89**
Liquid detergent	1 qt.	**2.78**

Food Shopping Problems

Group Discussion: Your Shopping Problems

Choose a note taker for your group to take notes on your discussion and to read the notes to the whole class afterwards.

1. Do you make a shopping list before you go shopping? Do you buy extra things? What extra things?
2. Do you ever waste money when you shop for food? What do you waste it on?
3. Did you ever run short of money at the checkout counter? What did you do?
4. Have you ever had any other problems shopping for food? Tell the group about them.

Partners' Role Play: Returning Spoiled Food

What is happening in this picture? Did anyone in your class ever buy milk that was sour? What other kinds of spoiled food have you bought? What did you say to the clerk when you returned it?

With your partner, decide on a kind of spoiled food, and role play returning it to the supermarket.

Metric and English Measurement

Class Discussion: Measurement Conversion

What is happening in this picture? Have you ever needed to convert metric to English measurements? English to metric? Make a list on the board of situations where you need to convert measurements.

Group Problem Solving: Converting Metric→English/English→Metric

Discuss the tables on the following pages with your teacher. Then use the tables to solve these problems with your group. Compare your answers with those of the class.

1. If a can of soup weighs 305 grams, how many ounces does it weigh?
2. If an aerosol can of bug spray is 12¾ ounces, how many grams does it weigh?
3. If a bottle of soda is two liters, how many quarts is it?
4. If a bag of cookies weighs 539 grams, how many ounces does it weigh?
5. If a wooden board measures three feet, how many meters is it?
6. If the store is two kilometers from your home, how many miles away is it?
7. You need two meters of cloth. How many yards do you ask for?
8. Your bedroom is 11′ by 13′. How many square meters of carpeting do you need?
9. How much do you weigh: in pounds? in kilograms?

English to Metric

Measures of Length

```
1 inch  = 25.4 millimeters
        = 2.54 centimeters
        = .0254 meter

1 foot  = .3 meter
1 yard  = .91 meter
1 mile  = 1.61 kilometers
```

To Remember:

12 in	= 1 ft
3 ft	= 1 yd
1760 yd	= 1 mi
5280 ft	= 1 mi

CONVERSIONS

When you know	Multiply by	to get
inches (in) (")	2.54	centimeters (cm)
feet (ft) (')	30	centimeters (cm)
yards (yd)	.91	meters (m)
miles (mi)	1.61	kilometers (km)

Measures of Area

```
1 square inch  = 6.45 square centimeters
1 square foot  =  .09 square meters
1 square yard  =  .84 square meters
1 square mile  = 2.59 square kilometers
```

CONVERSIONS

When you know	Multiply by	to get
square inches (in^2)	6.45	square centimeters (cm^2)
square feet (ft^2)	.09	square meters (m^2)
square yards (yd^2)	.84	square meters (m^2)
square miles (mi^2)	2.59	square kilometers (km^2)
acres	.4	hectares (ha)

Measures of Weight

```
1 ounce = 28.35 grams
1 pound = .45 kilogram
1 short = .91 metric ton
```

CONVERSIONS

When you know	Multiply by	to get
ounces (oz)	28.35	grams (g)
pounds (lb)	.45	kilograms (kg)
short tons (2000 lbs)	.91	metric tons (t)

Measures of Volume

1 cubic inch	=	16.39 cubic centimeters
1 cubic foot	=	.03 cubic meter
2 cubic yard	=	.76 cubic meter
1 cubic foot	=	28.32 liters

To Remember:

3 tsp = 1 Tbsp
2 c = 1 pt
4 c = 1 qt
4 qts = 1 gal

CONVERSIONS

When you know	Multiply by	to get
teaspoons (tsp)	5	milliliters (ml)
tablespoons (tbsp)	15	milliliters (ml)
fluid ounces (fl.oz)	30	milliliters (ml)
cups (c)	.24	liters (l)
pints (pt)	.47	liters (l)
quarts (qt)	.95	liters (l)
gallons (gal)	3.8	liters (l)
cubic feet (ft^3)	.03	cubic meters (m^3)
cubic yards	.76	cubic meters (m^3)

Measure of Liquid—Capacity

1 liquid quart	= .95 liter

CONVERSIONS

When you know	Multiply by	to get
liquid quarts (liq qt)	.95	liters (1)

Dry Measure—Capacity

1 dry quart	= 1.1 liters

CONVERSIONS

When you know	Multiply by	to get
dry quarts	1.1	liters (1)

Measures of Length

1 meter	= 39.37 inches
	= 3.28 feet
	= 1.09 yards
1 centimeter	= .4 inch
1 millimeter	= .04 inch
1 kilometer	= .62 mile

CONVERSIONS

When you know	Multiply by	to get
millimeters (mm)	.04	inches (in)
centimeters (cm)	.4	inches (in)
meters (m)	3.28	feet (ft)
meters (m)	1.09	yards (yd)
kilometers (km)	.62	miles (mi)

Measures of Area

1 square centimeter	= .16 square inches
1 square meter	= 10.76 square feet
	= 1.2 square yards
1 square kilometer	= .39 square mile

CONVERSIONS

When you know	Multiply by	to get
square centimeters (cm^2)	.16	square inches (in^2)
square meters (m^2)	1.2	square yards (yd^2)
square meters (m^2)	10.76	square feet (ft^2)
square kilometers (km^2)	.39	square miles (m^2)
hectares (ha) (10,000 m^2)	2.5	acres

Measures of Weight

1 gram	= .04 ounce
1 kilogram	= 2.2 pounds
1 metric ton	= 2204.62 pounds

CONVERSIONS

When you know	Multiply by	to get
grams	.035	ounces (oz)
kilograms (kg)	2.2	pounds (lb)
tonnes (100 kg) (t)	1.1	short tons

Measures of Volume

1 cubic centimeter	= .06 cubic inch
1 cubic meter	= 35.31 cubic feet
1 cubic meter	= 1.31 cubic yards
1 liter	= .04 cubic foot

CONVERSIONS

When you know	Multiply by	to get
milliliters (ml)	.03	fluid ounces (fl oz.)
liters (l)	2.1	pints (pt)
liters (l)	1.06	quarts (qt)
liters (l)	.26	gallons (gal)
cubic meters (m^3)	35.31	cubic feet (ft^3)
cubic meters (m^3)	1.31	cubic yards (yd^3)

Measure of Liquid—Capacity

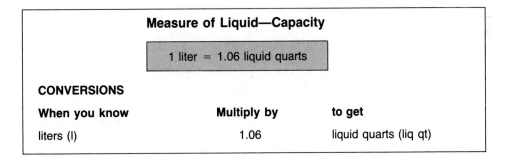

1 liter = 1.06 liquid quarts

CONVERSIONS

When you know	Multiply by	to get
liters (l)	1.06	liquid quarts (liq qt)

Dry Measure—Capacity

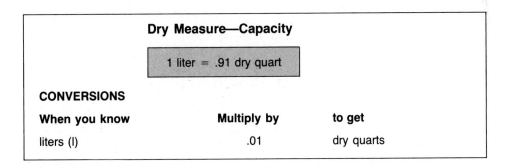

1 liter = .91 dry quart

CONVERSIONS

When you know	Multiply by	to get
liters (l)	.01	dry quarts

Shopping for Clothes

Partners' Role Play: Buying a Coat

Practice reading this dialog with your partner. Then role play the scene for your class.

Partners' Role Play: Buying a Sweater

Complete this dialog with your partner. Then practice reading it together. Finally, role play the scene for your class.

Group Activity: Important Questions to Ask

With your group, list as many important shopping questions as you can think of. Share your list with the rest of the class. Make a master list on the board.

What questions should you ask the salesperson when:

- you are buying a coat?
- you are buying shoes?
- you are buying a watch?
- you are buying a shirt?

_____

Group Discussion: Defective Clothing

Choose a note taker for your group to take notes on your discussion and to read the notes to the whole class afterwards.

1. What happened to the woman in this picture?
2. What should she do?
3. Did you ever buy some clothing and later find something wrong with it? What did you do about it?
4. Did you ever have trouble trying to return a defective item to a store? What happened?

Partners' Role Play: Returning Defective Clothing

With your partner, role play returning a defective piece of clothing to a store.

Layaway

Filling Out Forms: A Layaway Agreement

Fill out this layaway agreement with your partner.

1. Decide on something you would like to buy but don't have enough money for.
2. Decide how much money you can put down for a down payment.
3. Report on your agreement to the class.

Layaway Agreement

Name _____ Date _____

Address _____
          no.   street   city   state   zip

Phone number _____

Item _____

Initial payment _____

Date _____ _____

        _____ _____

        _____ _____

Total paid   _____

I agree to pay $ _____ every week and to pay in full within thirty days. If I do not fulfill this contract it is agreed that the merchandise will be returned to stock without further notice and my payments forfeited.

                           _____
                                 signature

Class Discussion: Your Merchandise on Layaway

Discuss these questions with your class.

1. Did you ever buy any merchandise on layaway?
2. What did you buy?
3. How many days did the store allow you to pay for it?
4. Which stores offer a layaway plan where you shop? What are the terms?
5. Is the layaway plan a good idea? Why or why not?
6. Are layaway plans popular in your native country? In what kinds of stores?

Bargains

Community Activity: Sales

Read about these sales with your class. At home or in class look through newspapers and fliers. Find one example of each type of sale. Compare your ads with other students' ads. Who found the most?

LUND'S

WHITE SALE

FINAL WEEK
SAVE 20 to 50%

SHEETS   TOWELS

BLANKETS   BEDSPREADS

TABLE LINENS   WASHABLE RUGS

MATTRESS PADS   STUDIO COVERS

PILLOWS

White sales are usually in the months of January and August. They are semiannual sales.

NOW THRU FRIDAY
AT **JASPER'S**
CLEARANCE SALE
25% OFF **ALL DRESSES**

A **clearance sale** helps the store clear the shelves and racks of merchandise before the new season. What other kind of sale is it like?

RICHARDSON'S COAT DEPT.

WAREHOUSE SALE

. . . WE'VE GATHERED ALL OUR BEAUTIFUL BUYS TOGETHER IN ONE LOCATION FOR A FINAL TWO DAY CLEARANCE SALE . . .

A **warehouse sale** is usually at the warehouse of a chain of stores. The sale is at the warehouse only.

GOING OUT OF BUSINESS SALE

Dining Room Sets 300⁰⁰

Mon–Fri
9:00 to 9:00

MAIN STREET FURNITURE STORE

EVERYTHING MUST GO!!

BEDROOM SETS 500⁰⁰

54 MAIN ST.
UTOPIA
566-4433

This store is closing. It won't open again. They want to sell everything at a going-out-of-business sale.

TIRES

- ALL SIZES
- ALL MAKES

CARLOS' TIRE STORE

CASH AND CARRY

Cash and carry means you pay cash (no checks or charges) and take the merchandise with you (no deliveries).

Is cash and carry a good idea in this sale?

Ordering from a Catalog

Community Activity: Order Blanks

Bring a store catalog to class. Fill in this order blank using the catalog. Order three items you need.

Order Blank

Name _____
            last   first   middle

Address _____
            no.   street   city   state   zip code

How shall we ship? (mark X)

Express ☐   Freight ☐   C.O.D. ☐
Pick up ☐   Parcel post ☐

Catalog Number	Quan.	Item	Color	Size	Wt.	Price

Total price

Postage & handling _____

Amount enclosed _____

or

Charge account number

Total shipping weight _____

_____

Check here for C.O.D. _____

Partners' Role Play: Ordering by Phone

Role play a telephone order with your partner.

Roles: Customer, telephone sales operator
Situation: Order the items on your order blank by telephone.

Guarantees

Group Discussion: Warranty

Choose a note taker for your group to take notes on your discussion and to read the notes to the whole class afterwards.

1. Did you ever buy anything with a guarantee? What did you buy?
2. What did the guarantee include? Parts? Labor? For how long?
3. Did you have to fill out and mail in a Warranty Card?
4. What is happening in the picture below? Do you own anything with a *lifetime guarantee*? What does a lifetime guarantee include?

Group Role Play: Complaining about a Guarantee

Discuss the scene above with your group. Choose two students to role play the situation for the class.

Class Activity: Your Guarantee and Warranty Card

Do you have a guarantee or warranty card from an item you bought? Bring one to class and discuss it.

Returns and Adjustments

Group Problem Solving: What to Do about Problems

What should you do if you are in one of the situations below? Discuss these problems, and report your group's solutions to the rest of the class.

Managing Your Money

Class Problem Solving: Deficit Spending

Read this problem with your class. With your class, answer the questions on the following page. Decide what the man should do.

HIS MONTHLY BUDGET:

Weekly take-home pay:	$255.
Monthly take-home pay (weekly × 4.3)	$1096.50

Fixed expenses
(monthly)

Rent	$300
Electric	50
Gas	25
Telephone	45
Insurance	180
Car loan payment	40
TV installment	30
Refrigerator installment	20
Furniture installment	45
Personal bank loan	45
TOTAL FIXED EXPENSES	$780

Monthly take-home	$1096.50
minus	–
Fixed expenses	$780.
Money left for variable expenses	$316.50

Variable expenses
(monthly)

Food	$400
Transporation	120
Clothing (charge account)	57
Medical	23
Dentist	65
TOTAL VARIABLE EXPENSES	$665.

Total expenses (fixed + variable)	1445.
Take-home pay	1096.50
Subtract **TOTAL EXPENSES**	– 1445.
Balance (take-home pay–expenses)	– $348.50

1. What will happen if he doesn't pay his telephone bill? His gas bill? His TV time payment? His bank loan payment? His dentist bill?
2. Which bills should he pay first?
3. Should he take out another loan to help pay these bills? Why or why not?
4. Should he pay part of each of the bills now and leave some for next month?
5. Should he declare bankruptcy?
6. How could he have avoided this situation?

Partners' Activity: Cutting Down Expenses

What are some ways to cut expenses and save money?

At home, to save on electricity, turn off lights.

To save on heat, keep the house cool.

Your idea.

Class Activity: Budgeting

Read this budget planning sheet with your class. Then fill in the blanks for your personal monthly budget.

Weekly take-home pay $ _____
(multiply by 4.3 for monthly take-home pay) $ _____

FIXED EXPENSES

(monthly; if not, multiply by 4.3)

Rent   _____

Electric   _____

Gas   _____

Telephone   _____

Insurance   _____

Car payments   _____

Other fixed: _____

                              _____

                              _____

TOTAL FIXED EXPENSES $ _____

VARIABLE EXPENSES

(monthly; if not, multiply by 4.3)

Food   _____

Transportation   _____

Clothing   _____

Medical   _____

Other: _____

TOTAL VARIABLE EXPENSES $ _____

TOTAL EXPENSES (fixed & variable) $ _____

BALANCE (take-home pay − expenses) $ _____

Consumer Complaints

Partners' Problem Posing: Letters of Complaint

What is happening in each of these pictures? Read the consumer information under each picture. With your partner, write a letter to complain about one of these problems. Read your letter to the class.

This man's lighter is unsafe. If he complains to the Consumer Product Safety Commission, they will find out more about the problem. If they think the lighters are unsafe, they will be taken off the market. If you buy something and you think it is unsafe in the United States, you can call the Commission (800-638-2666, or in Maryland 800-402-2937).

If you want to complain about food, drugs, additives, cosmetics, blood banks, sunlamps, or radiation from color TV's in the United States, write to the Food and Drug Administration, Department of Health, Education and Welfare, 5600 Fishers Lane, Rockville, Maryland 20852.

If you have a complaint about public transportation in the United States, you can write to the National Highway Traffic Safety Administration, Department of Transportation, 400 7th Street, Washington, D.C. 20590. They will help you with problems about safety in cars, buses, trucks, bicycles, motorcycles, and any other kind of motor vehicle or equipment related to it.

Values Clarification

Personal Values

Group Activity: Values

Add one value to the list below. Decide which of the values on this list are most important to you. Then label your most important value 1. Label the rest of the values 2 to 10. Finally, tell your group which value you selected as 1 and explain your choice.

If you have time, also explain the rest of your choices.

Satisfying work
Close family
World peace
Good health
Knowledge
Faith in God
Financial security
Freedom of opportunity
Nature
(Other) _____

Class Activity: Million Dollar Wish

What would you do if you had a million dollars? Write it on a piece of paper. Fold the paper and hand it in to your teacher. Listen as the teacher reads each answer, and try to guess who wrote it.

Find Someone Who . . .

Choose one of these things that you would like to do, or add another choice to the list. Then find someone else in your class who would like to do it too.

Tell the class what you picked and who else has the same wish.

Climb a mountain
Take a trip around the world
Go on a cruise
Be a professional athlete
Be a professional musician or singer
Buy a new car
Buy a house
Own a business
Move to a different place
Change to a different job
(Other) _____

Partners' Interview: Material Success

Ask your partner these questions. Then join a small group and compare your answers. Do people in your class have different ideas about success?

1. The couple in this picture would like to have a dishwasher. Are there any modern conveniences that you don't have and would like to have? What?
2. Are there any modern conveniences you already have that are very important to you? What?
3. Is material success important to you? Why or why not?
4. What material things would you have to have in order to feel successful?
5. What other kinds of success are important to you?
6. What do you think a person needs to become successful? (Luck? Ambition? Perseverance? A good education? Other . . .)
7. A "self-made" person is someone who starts with nothing and becomes very successful. Who are some famous self-made men and women? Do you admire them? Why or why not?

Group Discussion: Cross Cultural Values

Choose a note taker for your group to take notes on your discussion and to read the notes to the whole class afterwards.

1. A value is a belief or principle that is important to you. Are there any values that are important in your native country but do not seem so important to people in the United States? What are they?
2. Are there any values that seem to be more important to people in the United States than to people in your native country? What are they?
3. Do you think people's values change when they move to a different country? Why or why not?

Personal Journal

Keep a personal journal, a notebook in which you write your ideas about life. Write in it regularly. If you wish, share some of your journal entries with your teacher.

The Arts

Find Someone Who . . .

Find someone in your class who fits each description.

1. _____ paints pictures.

2. _____ plays a musical instrument.

3. _____ likes to sing.

4. _____ loves to dance.

5. _____ likes to draw.

6. _____ likes classical music.

7. _____ likes to act in plays.

8. _____ designs clothing.

9. _____ loves poetry.

10. _____ makes pottery.

11. _____ does woodworking.

12. _____ enjoys opera.

13. _____ sculpts.

14. _____ enjoys reading novels.

15. _____ likes to visit beautiful buildings.

16. _____ enjoys flower arranging.

17. _____ is a gourmet cook.

Class Project: Talent Show

Put on a talent show to showcase the talents in your class. Invite other students, families, and friends. Serve refreshments. Take photographs and write a news article on the talent show.

Class Discussion: The Arts

Discuss these pictures with your class. What is happening? What is the difference between being a spectator and an active participant in the arts?

Class Activity: Which Would You Rather Do?

It's a rainy weekend. Check three things on this list that you would like to do. Compare your choices with those of the class. Do students in your class prefer to be spectators or active participants in the arts? Which is the most popular art form in your class?

Spectators	Active Participants
1. Go to a concert	Play in a jam session
2. Go to a museum	Paint or draw a picture, or sculpt or make pottery
3. Listen to music at home	Sing or practice an instrument
4. Read a good book	Write a poem, a story, or a journal entry
5. Watch TV or go to a movie	Take photographs or make a home movie
6. Watch some kind of professional dancing	Go out dancing
7. (Other)_____	(Other) _____

Class Activity: Reading Poetry Aloud

Bring in a poem that you like and read it to the class. If the poem is not in English, tell the class what it means, or translate it into English.

Look in the poetry section of the library to find an English poem that you like. Copy it down, bring it to class, and give it to the teacher. Listen as the teacher reads all the poems aloud, and choose the one you like the best. Memorize it, and recite it for the class.

Group Decision Making: Funding the Arts

You are on the board of trustees for a Foundation for the Arts. Every year your foundation provides funding for two special projects. This year there are four final proposals for you to choose from. Make your decision, and report to the class.

1. Fund a summer camp for local young people who are talented in music, dance, drama, or writing.
2. Commission wall paintings and sculpture by local artists to redecorate your City Hall, which was damaged in a fire this year.
3. Provide five four-year scholarships for local high school graduates to continue their study in five areas of the arts: music, dance, art, architecture, and theater.
4. Fund an arts series that will bring internationally famous artists to perform locally.

Class Trip: Art Appreciation

Would your class like to go together to visit a museum or attend a special artistic performance? What museums, shows, or concerts are available in your area? Look in the newspaper for ideas, and decide together.

High Technology

Find Someone Who . . .

Find someone in your class who fits each description. Share your answers with the class.

1. _____ has a digital watch.
2. _____ has a calculator.
3. _____ has a color television.
4. _____ has used a computer.
5. _____ has used a video cassette recorder.
6. _____ has an instant camera.
7. _____ has used a cordless telephone.
8. _____ has used an answering machine.
9. _____ has used a microwave oven.
10. _____ has a mini-cassette recorder with earphones.

Class Discussion: High-Technology Office

Discuss this picture with your class. Would you like to work in this office? Why or why not? Do you use high technology in your job now? Tell the class about it.

Poll the Class: Hi-Tech Attitudes

Which of these statements express the way you feel about high technology? Poll the class, and see how many students choose each answer. Does your class like high technology or not?

	Yes	No
I am interested in studying high technology.		
I like to use high-technology products.		
I don't trust high technology.		
I don't have anything to do with high technology.		
I'm not sure what I think of high technology.		

Group Discussion: Hi-Tech Experiences

Choose a note taker for your group to take notes on your discussion and to read the notes to the whole class afterwards.

1. Did you ever have trouble trying to use a new machine?
2. What is your favorite high-technology invention?
3. Did you ever have an experience with a computer error? What did you do?
4. Imagine the world one hundred years in the future. What changes do you think high technology will have made by then?

Environment

Class Problem Posing: Pollution

Match the names of these problems with the pictures below. Which of these kinds of pollution is the biggest problem in the area where you live now? Is anything being done to correct it? What can be done?

Water pollution   Noise pollution
Littering   Air pollution

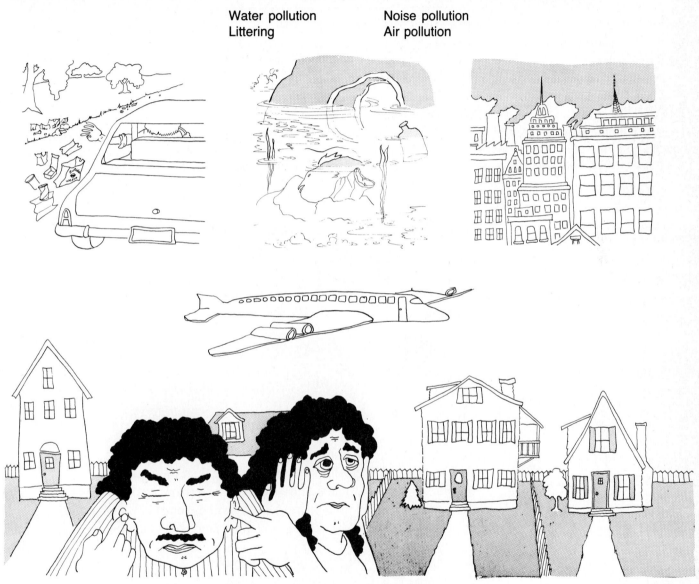

Community Activity: Articles on Environmental Hazards

Look in newspapers or magazines for articles on environmental problems. Bring an article to class and discuss it with a small group. Report your discussion to the class.

Poll the Class: Nuclear Power

Take an opinion poll of your class on these nuclear power issues. Write the results on the board. Discuss the results.

	Approve	Disapprove	No Opinion
Defensive nuclear weapons in space			
Nuclear weapons freeze			
Nuclear arms limitation treaties between the U.S.A. and U.S.S.R.			
Nuclear power to generate electricity			

Group Decision-Making: Overpopulation

You are the members of the Ministry of Health in a third-world country. Overpopulation is a growing problem in your country. The head of your government has selected you to find a solution to this problem. Some suggestions are listed below. You may use any of them or add others. Prepare a plan and report it to the class.

Suggestions:

1. Pay parents *not* to have babies.
2. Require a head tax for families with more than two children.
3. Pay men who volunteer to be sterilized by means of a vasectomy.
4. Pay women who volunteer to be sterilized by means of a tubal ligation.
5. Provide free birth control pills and other birth control devices for women and men.
6. Provide public education on birth control.
7. Provide free abortion clinics for women.
8. Make it illegal for anyone to have more than two children.

Class Discussion: Natural Disasters

Match the names of these natural disasters with the pictures. Discuss the pictures with your class. Write down the new vocabulary you need to use to talk about them. What other natural disasters are there?

Hurricane	Flood	Earthquake
Tornado	Drought	Forest Fire
Tidal wave	Volcano	Insect Plague

152

Speech: Natural Disasters in My Native Country

Which of these natural disasters occur in your native country? Tell the class about them. Answer these questions in your speech. Use the Speech and Audience Evaluation Forms on page 175 of the Appendix.

1. What happens in these disasters? (Be specific. If you have ever experienced one, describe it.)
2. What do people do when these natural disasters occur?
3. What does the government do to prepare for or prevent these disasters?

Class Activity: Endangered Species and Destruction of Natural Resources

Make two lists on the board, including all of the endangered species of animals and endangered natural resources that you can think of. Find information in the library about these species and resources. If possible, ask a guest speaker to talk to your class on these problems.

Endangered Species   Natural Resources

Group Problem Solving: Preservation of Wildlife and Conservation of Natural Resources

Choose one of these problems to discuss with your group. Present your solution to the class.

1. It is illegal to kill American bald eagles because they are an endangered species. Nevertheless, some farmers are still killing the eagles because the eagles kill their young livestock. What can be done to preserve the eagles and protect the livestock?

2. It is illegal to kill alligators because they are an endangered species. Nevertheless, hunters are still killing the alligators to make money, since people like to wear shoes and belts made of alligator skin. What can be done?

3. Strip mining turns good land into wastelands, yet it provides us with important minerals. What can be done to protect the land and provide the minerals?

Group Problem Posing: Worst Problem of the World

Choose the three worst problems the world faces today from this list and number them 1, 2, 3. (You may add another problem to the list if you wish.) Compare your choices with those of the rest of your group. As a group, choose one problem that you think is the worst. Report your choice to the class, and explain why you chose that problem.

International terrorism
Overpopulation
Nuclear weapons
Environmental pollution
Destruction of natural resources
(Other) _____

Crime and Punishment

Class Discussion: What Would You Do?

What is happening in these pictures? What should you do if you are the victim?

Group Activity: Crime Prevention

How can these crimes be prevented? Make a list of suggestions with your group. Share your list with the class.

- Mugging
- Car theft
- Kidnapping
- Child abuse
- Rape

Group Activity: Police Protection

Discuss these questions and report to the class.

1. Have you ever had any contact with the police? What happened?
2. What do police officers do where you live now?
3. How do you feel about the police in your community? Check whether you agree or disagree with each of the statements following. Discuss your choices with your group.

	Agree	Disagree
Most police are honest.		
Police do an important job for society.		
People don't appreciate the hard work that police do.		
Police should be paid more money, so that they won't be tempted to take bribes.		
What some poeple call "police brutality" is usually necessary for self-defense.		
Police salaries are too high.		
Many police are dishonest.		
I am afraid of police brutality.		
Police often use their guns too quickly.		
Police often treat teenagers unfairly.		
Police often treat minorities unfairly.		

Class Discussion: Capital Punishment

Capital punishment is the death penalty. It is legal in the United States. Is it legal in your native country? Do you approve or disapprove? Why? Do you think capital punishment is ever justified? When?

Community Activity: Capital Punishment Survey

Take a survey of the opinions of other students and teachers at your school. Each student in your class should ask five people outside the class this question:

Do you approve of capital punishment?

	Yes	No	Not Sure
1.			
2.			
3.			
4.			
5.			

Report your responses to the class. Add up the class results on the board. What did your survey show? Discuss the results.

Poll the Class: Prisons

How do your classmates feel about the prison (penal) system? Poll the class and find out.

	Agree	Disagree
Rehabilitation of criminal offenders is an important task for society.		
Rehabilitation programs for adult criminals are a waste of time and money.		
Prison conditions should be improved. Prisoners should be treated more fairly.		
Prison sentences aren't effective because convicted criminals can be paroled too easily.		
Prison sentences are unfair because minorities get tougher sentences.		

Citizenship

Class Activity: National Anthem

This is the national anthem of the United States. It was written during the War of 1812. Have you ever heard it? Where? Can anyone in your class sing it? Read the words together.

What is the national anthem of your native country? Sing it for the class if you can and tell what the words mean. When is it used in your native country?

THE STAR-SPANGLED BANNER

Class Discussion: Voting

Discuss these questions with your class.

1. This is a picture of a polling place in the United States. Does it look the same as a polling place in your native country? What is the same? What is different?
2. If officials are not elected in your native country, how are they chosen?
3. How many major political parties are there in your native country? What are their names? Is the government formed from a single party or a coalition of parties?
4. How often are elections held in your native country? When are they held?
5. Have you ever voted in an election? Have you ever campaigned for a candidate? Did your candidate win? Tell the class about it.

Community Activity: Heads of Government

Find this information and bring it to class. (If you are living in the United States, do 1-7; if not, do 1-3.) Compare notes with your classmates.

1. The name of the President of the U.S.A. _____
2. The name of the Vice-President of the U.S.A. _____
3. The name of the head of the government in your native country _____
4. The name of two U.S. senators from the state you live in _____
5. The name of the U.S. Representative from your district _____
6. The name of the governor of your state _____
7. The name of the head or heads of your city or town government _____

158

Group Discussion: Government

Choose a note taker for your group to take notes on your discussion and to read your notes to the whole class afterwards.

1. Is the government of your native country military or civilian?
2. How long has the present government of your native country been in power?
3. Was the previous government of your country similar to the present government? If not, how was it different?
4. Does your native country have a constitution? Is it important to the government?
5. How do you feel about politics? What kind of government do you think is best?
6. Has there ever been a revolution in your native country? When?
7. What do you like about the government of the country you live in now? Would you like to be involved in it?
8. What does the flag of your native country look like? Draw a picture of it and explain it to your group.

Find Someone Who . . .

From the list below, check three ways you prefer to help other people. (You may add another). Then find someone else in the class who made the same choices.

Volunteer to help in a hospital

Give money every week at a church

Donate money to a charity

Give money to a beggar on a street

Volunteer to help raise money for a charity

Help someone who is old

Take a homeless person into your home

(Other) _____

Group Role Play: Responsive Government

Choose one of these situations, or add your own community problem, and role play it with your group for the class.

1. You are a group of parents. There is no playground for the children in your neighborhood, so they play in the street. Recently, one of the children was hit by a car and seriously injured. Meet with the mayor to petition for a playground in your neighborhood.
2. You are a group of neighbors. There is a dangerous intersection on your street. Almost every week there is a car or motorcycle accident at this intersection. Take a petition signed by 50 neighbors to a City Council meeting to demand a stop light at this intersection.
3. You are a group of concerned citizens. Your state wants to build a toxic waste disposal plant in your town. You are worried about the danger of poisonous chemicals leaking. Meet with the governor of your state to protest this action.

Community Activity: Public Meetings

With a partner, attend a public meeting of some branch of the local government where you live. Report to your class on the meeting. (NOTE: Notices of public meetings will be listed in local newspapers. You can also call City Hall for information.)

Class Discussion: Pledge of Allegiance

Children in the United States learn this pledge of allegiance in school. New citizens must pledge allegiance to the flag of the United States when they are naturalized. What does the pledge mean? Do you think it is a good idea? Is there a similar pledge in your native country?

*I pledge allegiance to the
flag of the United States
of America, and to the
republic for which it stands,
one nation, under God, indivisible,
with liberty and justice for all.*

Speech: Government Of Your Native Country

Prepare a brief speech for your class about the government of your native country. If everyone is from the same country, talk about different parts of the government. Practice with a small group before you present your speech to the class. You may use note cards but do not read your speech. Use the speech and audience evaluation forms on page 175 of the Appendix.

Ethnic Identity

Partners' Interview: Ethnic Identity

Ask your partner these questions. Report your interview to the class.

1. What is your "ethnic background"? (Where are your parents, grandparents, ancestors from?)
2. What ethnic customs and traditions does your family keep? (Food? Religion? Language? Holidays? Music? Family life?)
3. What ethnic groups make up the population of your native country? Is it an ethnic "melting pot" like the United States?
4. Do you think it is important to keep any traditions from your native country or ethnic group? Why or why not?
5. Which customs from your native country do people follow when they live in the United States? Which customs do they change? Why?
6. In your native country, are there ethnic districts in different parts of the country? What ethnic groups live in them?
7. Do you live in an ethnic neighborhood now? What ethnic group, or groups, live there?
8. Have many people from your native country emigrated to the United States? Why have they emigrated? Where do they usually live in the United States? Do they like living in the United States? Why, or why not?

Community Activity: Visit to an Ethnic District

Go with your class to visit an ethnic district in your town, and eat in an ethnic restaurant. If possible, go on a day when an ethnic festival is being celebrated. Enjoy yourselves!

Group Activity: Cross-Cultural Advice Column

You are advice columnists for the local newspaper. You call yourselves Aunt Mary. People write letters to you, asking for advice, and you write answers to them in the newspaper. Decide as a group how to answer these letters. Read your advice to the class.

> *Dear Aunt Mary,*
>
> *My family and I have been living in the United States for three years. We like it here, but now we have a problem. My husband and I always speak our native language at home and keep the customs of our old country, because we don't want our children to forget their cultural heritage. But our children want to speak English at home now, and they seem to be embarrassed by our customs. Sometimes I think they want to forget where they came from! My husband and I are very upset about this. What can we do?*
>
> *Miserable Mother*

> *Dear Aunt Mary,*
>
> *I am in love with an American girl, and she is in love with me. We both want to get married, but the problem is our parents. They are very angry and refuse to give us their blessing. They think we cannot have a good marriage simply because we have different cultural and religious backgrounds. (I am a Moslem from Syria, and my fiancée is Jewish.) We love our parents and do not want to disappoint them, but we feel we have the right to make our own choice. We really love each other very much! Please help us!*
>
> *Desperate Lover*

161

> *Dear Aunt Mary,*
>
> *I'm a foreign student studying in the United States, and I've been living here for almost a year. My problem is loneliness. I've been studying English, and I can speak it pretty well now, but I can't seem to make friends here. I feel shy and depressed most of the time, and I miss my family and friends at home.*
>
> *Homesick in Haverhill*

Community Interview: Ethnic Heritage

Use these questions to interview someone in your community. Take notes, and report your interview to the class.

1. What country, or countries, did your ancestors come from?
2. What has your family kept of that ethnic heritage?
3. Have you ever visited the country or countries your ancestors came from?
4. What ethnic group do you consider yourself as being a part of?
5. What are the special characteristics of your ethnic group? What do you like best about it?

Ethnic Stereotypes

Group Activity: Stereotypes of Ethnic Groups

A stereotype is a generalized idea of what everyone in a certain group looks like or acts like. Stereotypes are always too general and too simple to be realistic. Do you recognize any of the stereotypes below? Match the pictures with the ethnic groups. Then discuss how you recognized the stereotypes. Do you think there is any truth to any of these stereotypes? Report your discussion to the class.

American Indian	Mexican	Greek
Black American	Italian	Hawaiian
Japanese	Eskimo	Chinese

Group Discussion: Stereotyping

Choose a note taker for your group to take notes on your discussion and to read the notes to the whole class afterwards.

1. Do any members of your group belong to any of these ethnic groups? Do they fit the stereotypes?

2. Do you know any other people who seem to fit these stereotypes? Any people who don't?

3. Is there any truth at all in any of these stereotypes? What do the stereotypes come from?

4. In your native country, what stereotyped ideas do people have about Americans? About other foreigners?

5. Sometimes stereotyping can make people prejudiced against each other. This can cause serious problems. Can you think of any examples?

6. Comedy is often based on stereotypes. There are many stereotyped characters in television comedies and people laugh at them. Who are some stereotyped TV characters?

7. Did you ever watch a television series from the United States in your native country? What show?

8. Did the show stereotype Americans? Did you believe any of the stereotypes?

9. If you have been to the United States, was it what you expected? What was the same? What was different?

Partners' Problem Solving: Discrimination

Read these problems with your class, and discuss them with your partner. What would you do in each case?

1. The woman in this picture wants to rent an apartment, but the landlord refuses to rent to her. She feels he is discriminating against her. What should she do? What would you do?

2. You are walking down the street when a stranger bumps into you and calls you a bad name because of your race or ethnic background. What should you do? What would you probably do?

3. At your work, one of the other employees frequently says offensive things about your race, sex, or ethnic group. The other employees tell you not to pay any attention to it, but it really bothers you. What should you do? What would you probably do?

Class Discussion: Whose Is the Land?

Many native American Indian tribes have been trying for a long time to get back lands that the United States promised to them in treaties. In 1883 a great Sioux Indian leader, Sitting Bull (Tatanka Yotanka), explained why the Indians were trying to get back the land. He said:

> "If a man loses anything and goes back and looks carefully for it he will find it, and that is what the Indians are doing now when they ask you to give them the things that were promised them in the past; and I do not consider that they should be treated like beasts."

Do you think that the United States should give back these lands that it promised long ago? Why, or why not?

In your native country, has there ever been a fight for the land between different ethnic groups? What happened? Tell the class about it.

Education

Group Discussion: Classroom Informality

These are pictures of American college classrooms. Compare them with college classrooms in your native country. Share your comparisons with the class.

Partners' Interview: Educational Systems

Ask your partner these questions. Report your interview to the class.

1. In American schools, there is much emphasis on writing. Most tests are written. How are tests taken in your native country?

2. Does your city or town provide bilingual education? In what languages? What are some advantages and disadvantages of bilingual education?

3. In American education, emphasis is placed on problem solving and discussion. If students have different opinions from those of their teachers they are encouraged to express them and explain their reasoning. In your native country, is there emphasis on practical problem solving? Is there much class discussion?

4. Are students required to do more or less memorizing of information in your native country than in the United States?

5. In the United States, children are required to attend school until they are sixteen years old. Is education compulsory in your native country? How many years of school are required?

6. What are some differences between high schools in the United States and schools in your native country?

7. Compare the educational systems in your native country and the United States. What are the strengths and weaknesses of each system?

Group Decision Making: Hiring a New Teacher

Imagine you are members of a school committee. You are meeting to decide whom to hire as a high school history teacher. Read the descriptions, discuss, and decide as a group which one to hire. Explain your decision to the class.

1. Martin Albert; 32; unmarried white American; has bachelor's degree, master's degree, doctoral degree from excellent university with high honors; has taught for 6 years; brings with him excellent references from former students; lost his last job when he admitted he was a homosexual and joined a gay rights organization; students said he never mentioned it in class.

2. Maria Santana-Martinez; 34; native of Peru; naturalized citizen of the U.S.; married with two children; has bachelor's degree and master's degree from university in Peru; taught in bilingual program for two years; left job when husband changed jobs and they moved; speaks with a Spanish accent, but can usually be understood well in English.

3. John Colson; 56; black American; has bachelor's and master's degrees from state teacher's college; widower with three children—two of his children are in college; has taught for 34 years; brings with him excellent recommendations from former students; lost his former job when all the teachers were fired because of a teacher strike—says he joined the strike because he believed in it.

Group Decision Making: School Budget

Imagine you are school administrators. You must cut one major item from your school budget for next year. Which of these items will you eliminate? Report your decision to the class and justify it.

- Music teacher
- Biology lab microscopes
- Sports program
- Roof repair
- Computer for administrative purposes

Partners' Problem Solving: Parent–Teacher Conferences

In most American schools, teachers ask parents to come to school for parent–teacher conferences several times each year. The teacher and parents discuss the child's progress in school as well as any problems. Discuss these problems with your partner. Choose one situation. Write a dialog. Practice role playing the dialog, then present it to the class.

1. Mary, eight years old, is very shy and afraid of going to school. She gets a stomach ache and cries every morning when it is time to go to school.

2. Peter, ten years old, is a discipline problem. He fights in the schoolyard and talks back to the teacher.

3. Ann, eleven years old, is very bright and is bored with the school work her teacher is giving her.

4. Jimmy is nine years old. He is a slow learner and the teacher thinks he should be retained in the fourth grade for another year. He doesn't want to. He is upset by the idea of having to stay back.

5. John is fourteen years old. He has been skipping school. His parents thought he was going to school every day, but he has actually been going to his friend's house.

Community Activity: Education in Your Community

Look in the newspaper for an article about education in your community. Cut out the article. Read it. Report on it to the class.

Evaluation

Partners' Interview: Oral Evaluation

Choose a topic that you would like to talk about. Write five to ten questions on the topic for your partner to ask you. Present your interview to the class or video tape the interview. Use the oral fluency evaluation form on page 174 in the Appendix to evaluate your communicative competency in the interview.

Group Activity: Self-Evaluation

In some courses, teachers ask students to evaluate their own learning. Answer these questions for yourself. Share your answers with your group and your teacher.

1. What did you learn in this course?
2. Do you feel good about your effort in this course? If you could take the course again, would you study more? Less? The same amount? The same way?
3. How do you feel about your English now? What do you need to work on?

Writing Activity: Course Evaluation

At the end of many courses for adults in the United States, the teacher asks the students to evaluate the course and make suggestions for the future. Answer these questions for your teacher. Try to answer honestly. Your answers will help your teacher to plan for the next term.

1. What was the best thing about this course?
2. What do you think your teacher should do the same way next term?
3. What do you think your teacher should change next term?
4. Do you think there should be more homework? Less homework? The same homework?
5. Do you think there should be more tests? Fewer tests? The same number of tests?

Appendix

City and Country: Pictures to Compare

City apartment has:

apartment building
elevator
fire escape
window boxes
balcony
recreation room
compactor
laundry room
storeroom
three floors
window locks
garage
sidewalk
furnishings
TVs, pool table,
chairs, mirror, washing
machines, lamp, bed,
tables, rug, pictures

_____
_____
_____

Country home has:

single family house
yard
fence with gate
trees
pets (dog and cat)
two stories
flower bed
fieldstone chimney and foundation
shutters
vegetable garden
tomatoes
pumpkins
porch light
rocking chair
porch

_____
_____
_____

CARS: Pictures to compare

two-door convertible sports car
stereo
cassette player
automatic transmission
antenna
luxury hubcaps
covered headlights
bucket seats
oversized side mirrors
dent in front fender

_____

four-door sedan
two tone
manual transmission
standard hubcaps
glove compartment
door locks
exhaust pipe
tail lights

170

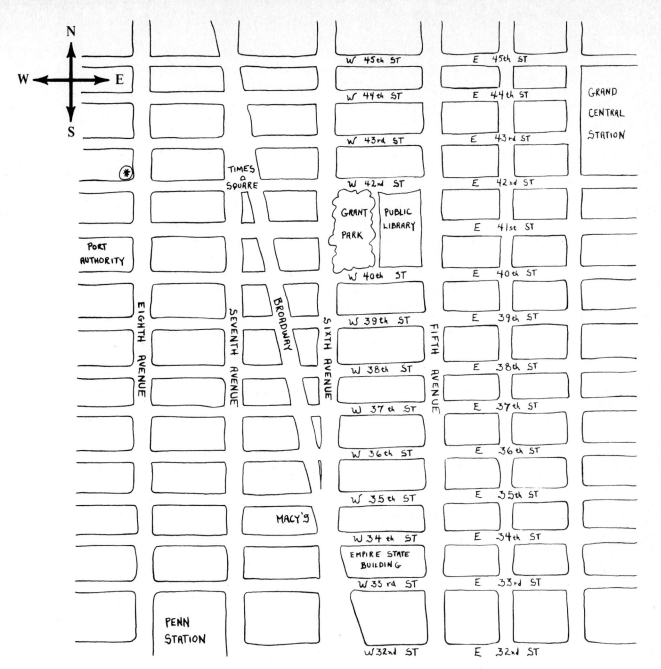

MAP READING ANSWERS

1. To get to Times Square, walk one block east on 42nd street.

2. To get to Macy's from Eighth and 42nd, walk one block east to Times Square; then walk seven blocks south on Broadway.

3. To get to the Empire State building from Eighth and 42nd, walk one block east to Times Square; then walk one more block east to Sixth Avenue. Walk eight blocks south to 34th Street.

4. To get to the Public Library from Eighth and 42nd, walk straight on 42nd Street for three blocks.

5. To get to Penn Station from Eighth and 42nd, walk south on Eighth Avenue for nine blocks.

1. Dog bite: Wash wound with soap and water. Try to keep the animal; don't destroy it. It must be tested for rabies. Call the doctor.
2. Aspirin overdose: Call the doctor. Bring child to the hospital.
3. Snakebite: Contact a doctor. Keep the victim motionless. Place a wide tourniquet above the bite. Tighten it enough for one finger to pass beneath with difficulty. Loosen and move the tourniquet up each hour if there is swelling. Then tighten. Place an ice pack on the swelling.
4. Sunburn: Take a cool bath or shower. Drink cold drinks. Use cold cream or oil on skin.
5. Bee sting: Apply a pack of baking soda and water. Be careful removing the stinger. Apply ice. If patient has a bad reaction, call the doctor.
6. Cinder in eye: Wash with clean, running water. Pull upper lid over lower. If the eye becomes irritated and the cinder does not come out, contact the doctor.
7. Nosebleed: Keep patient in sitting position with his head back. Loosen clothing around neck. Keep cold, wet cloths over the nose. If bleeding doesn't stop in a few minutes, call the doctor.
8. Fainting: Lower the head or raise the legs. Loosen tight clothing. If patient doesn't recover in a few minutes, call the doctor.
9. Poison ivy: Wash with soap and water. For a mild case, use calamine lotion. For a severe case, see the doctor.

The Human Body

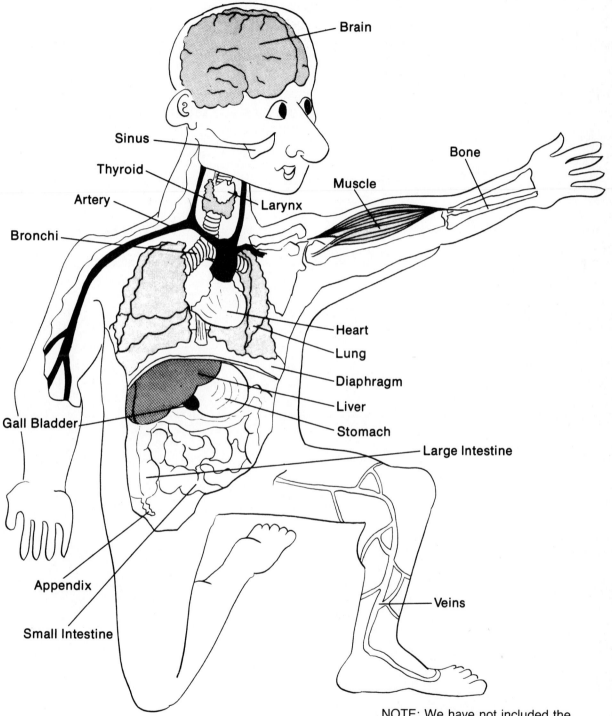

Brain

Sinus

Thyroid

Artery

Bronchi

Gall Bladder

Appendix

Small Intestine

Larynx

Bone

Muscle

Heart

Lung

Diaphragm

Liver

Stomach

Large Intestine

Veins

NOTE: We have not included the excretory and reproductive systems of the human body in this book because they are not topics of polite conversation in the United States.

173

ORAL COMMUNICATION EVALUATION FORM

Student's Name _____

Date: _____

Scale:

1: Frequent noticeable difficulty; interferes with communication
3: Occasional difficulty; interferes slightly with communication
5: Satisfactory competency for level; comfortable communication with
   native-English speakers.

****

	ACCEPTABLE/ SUFFICIENT	INTERFERES SLIGHTLY WITH COMMUNICATION	INTERFERES WITH COMMUNICATION/ INSUFFICIENT
PRONUNCIATION	5	3	1
FLUENCY (ease of speaking)	5	3	1
WORD ORDER (grammar)	5	3	1
VOCABULARY	5	3	1
LISTENING COMPREHENSION	5	3	1
TOTALS:	_____ +	_____ +	_____ =

OVERALL TOTAL:

$\times\ 4$

%

Evaluator: _____

Comments: _____

_____

You may make as many copies of these forms as is necessary.

SPEECH EVALUATION FORM

Speaker's Name: _____

Date: _____

Speech Topic: _____

	Needs Work	Satisfactory
Organization		
Pronunciation		
Vocabulary		
Eye Contact		
Visual Aids		
Best Part of Speech		

Best Part of Speech

Evaluator

AUDIENCE EVALUATION FORM

Speaker's Name: _____

Date: _____

Speech Topic: _____

	Needs Work	Satisfactory
Attentiveness		
Quietness		
Eye Contact		
Appropriateness of Questions		
Form of Questions		
Number of Questions		
Responsiveness		
Evaluator